WHATCOM PLACES II

Beauty is in the eye of the beholder. That familiar saying is partially true—what we see filters through our emotions, our lives and our individual needs. The best land use in Whatcom County is viewed differently by a biologist, a realtor, an unemployed family from Detroit, an immigrant from Mexico, or someone raised in Van Zandt; the tree-lined parkway that one person admires blocks a water view cherished by another. Yet to say that beauty is a matter of opinion remains only partially true. At times we can all rejoice together in the beauty we behold: a summer sunset from Semiahmoo, Mount Baker on a cold winter morning above Hannegan Road farmland, the universal appeal of Mount Shuksan from Picture Lake. The trick in building community is to learn from our differences and to share our common visions.

WHATCOM LAND TRUST
Preserving the *Nature* of Whatcom County

A large Sitka spruce *(Picea sitchensis)* rises above Nooksack River salmon habitat, saved by the people who bought *Whatcom Places*. Part of your purchase price of this book will help conserve such land.

Photo: Eric Carabba

1

"Panta rhei" (Everything flows.)

Heraclitus, 6th century B.C.

Photo: Jon Brunk

Published by the Whatcom Land Trust

P.O. Box 6131

Bellingham, Washington 98227

(360) 650-9470

whatcomlandtrust.org

CONTRIBUTORS

Generosity and encouragement from the following business firms, foundations and individuals made this second edition possible. Whatcom Land Trust appreciates their partnership.

Anvil Corporation

Julie Carpenter Real Estate, Inc.

Barron Smith Daugert, PLLC, Attorneys

Kirsten Barron & Steve Brinn

Blythe Plumbing & Heating

BP Cherry Point Refinery

Brett Baunton/Artscan

Brown & Cole Stores

The Cascade Joinery

Joan Casey & John Watts

Community Food Co-op

ConocoPhillips Ferndale Refinery

Copies Now

Dutch Mothers Restaurant

Everybody's Store

Exxel Pacific

Fairhaven Village Inn

Fourth Corner Nurseries

The Greenhouse

Greg Aanes Furniture

Harmony Motor Works

Lithtex Northwest

Mark Anderson Land Company

Metcalf Hodges P.S.

Suzette & Craig Moore

Morse Steel Service

Mount Baker Automotive Parts & Service

Gary & Patricia Nelson

Northwest Propane LLC

Raincountry Refrigeration

RMC Architects

Roderick C. Burton–Art &Design

Phyllis & Charles Self Fund at the Whatcom Community Foundation

South Fork Construction

Douglas Tolchin

Tom's Bamboo

Trillium Corporation

Bob & Betty Tull

Village Books

Sid & Aline Wanne

Waycross Investment Management Company

Whatcom Community Foundation

Wilder Construction Company, Inc.

Wood Stone Corporation

The unmistakable fragrance of invasive blackberries *(Rubus discolor)* pervades Whatcom County in late summer.
Photo: Gloria Ruyle

Our thanks to many individuals for advice and help in the planning, funding, and production of Whatcom Places *and* Whatcom Places II:

Mike Abendhoff, Mark Anderson, Jeff Arvin, Mark Bender, Merrill Bevan, Harte Bressler, Connie Clement, Jerry DeBacker, Kevin DeVries, Patricia Hixon, Rand Jack, Pat Karlberg, Troy Luginbill, Jeff McClure, Lindsey McGuirk, Bob Morse, Kevin Murphy, Kathleen Pennington, Russ Pfeiffer-Hoyt, Mike and Barbara Ryan, Bill Sargeant, Bruce Smith, David Syre, Steve VanderYacht, Mark Vondrachek

Whatcom Places II *Book Committee:*
Bob Keller, chair; Brett Baunton, Rod Burton, Dean Kahn, Ginger Oppenheimer, Chuck Robinson, Helen Scholtz, Connie Shannon, Scott Wheeler

PHOTOGRAPHERS

The Land Trust recognizes the important role of outstanding photographers in protecting nature. We are thankful for their cooperation in making this book possible.

Brett Baunton
Mark Bergsma
Marcy Bloomenthal
Matt Brown
Jon Brunk
Bob Butterfield
Eric Carabba
Gene Davis
Manuel Rod del Pozo
Jonathan Duncan
Tim Fitzharris
Jason Glover
Sharon Eva Grainger
Kevin Kelliher
Lee Mann
Margaretha Maryk
Dick McNeely

Chris Moench
Grant Myers
Charles Nishida
Tore Ofteness
Ginger Oppenheimer
Patrick Reeves
Gloria Ruyle
Steve Satushek
Helen Scholtz
Gordon Scott
John Scurlock
Fredrick Sears
Bob and Ira Spring
Jon Timmer
Mark Turner
Roger Weiss
Ann Yow

Thanks to many others who helped provide images:
The Bellingham Herald
Farm Friends
Port of Bellingham
The Nature Conservancy
Nooksack Salmon Enhancement Association
North Cascades Institute
Whatcom Museum of History and Art

Cascade foothills meet autumn woodlands along Goodwin
Road in northeastern Whatcom County.

Photo: Manuel Rod del Pozo

A SENSE OF PLACE

One dusk I squinted across the land where I was growing up and saw that the prairie is really a seascape.

The wind was blowing, as it did day and night that summer, and the moving waves of rich-yellow wheat could just be seen in the settling dark. A harvesting combine cruised on the far side of the field. I had never been within a thousand miles of an ocean, but I knew that the combine, with its running lights just flicked on, was a freighter bound through the night for Sydney. Bench hills rose to the north, surely a fair coastline. The expanse of it all, hills and fields and wind in the wheat, extended like an ocean to where the sky and the flat horizon fitted together.

The magic of place is indelible. I was fifteen, there at that found sea which was both fictional and real. Now at 57 I write about both the Montana land where I grew up and the Puget Sound country where I have spent the majority of my years. Always I have believed that writers of caliber must ground their work in specific land and lingo in order to write of that larger country, life. So it is with us all, I would argue. Richard Hugo, the great poet of Montana and Washington, had a saying that sounded to me like something he picked up one especially grand night in a Missoula bar: "If you ain't noplace, you can't go nowhere." To have a base, a plot of accustomed existence on this earth, to be familiar with its changes of the seasons—there is propulsive rhythm to that. The ultimate experiencing of a sense of place comes from grounding our lives in such specific gifts of earth, and in having the sense to preserve them.

Ivan Doig

Ivan Doig was born in White Sulphur Springs, Montana, in 1939. His first book, the highly acclaimed memoir This House of Sky, *was a finalist for the National Book Award. In 1989, the Western Literature Association honored him with its Distinguished Achievement Award for his body of work.*

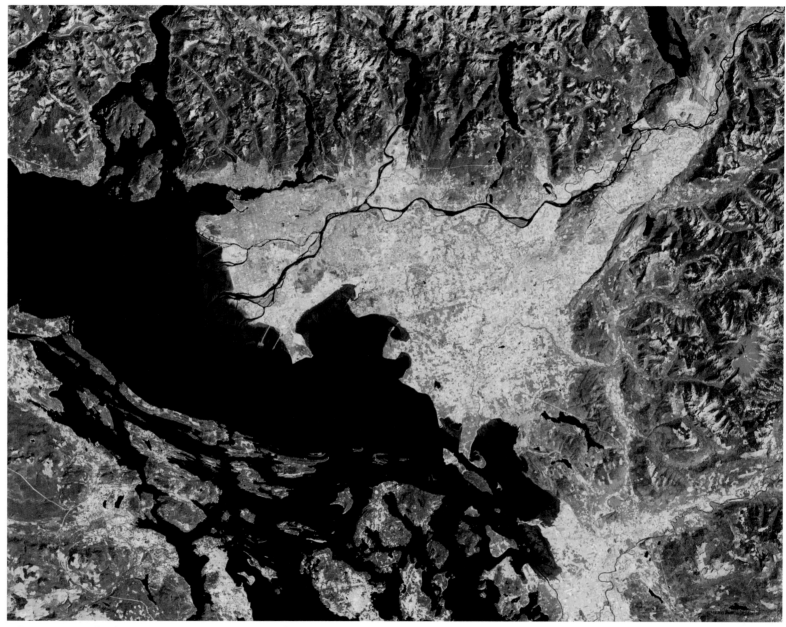

Whatcom County lies between two major river systems: the Fraser (north) and Skagit (south) as seen in this Landsat photo of Vancouver Island (bottom left), the Strait of Georgia, the San Juan Islands (bottom center), lower mainland B.C., and western Whatcom County.

Nature delights in design.
Photo: Grant Myers

CONTENTS

A Sacred Place, *William Dietrich* 8

Whatcom Places, *Robert Keller* 11

Shorelines, *Dave Peebles* 19

Rugged and Roadless, *Wendy Walker* 39

Foothills, *Binda Colebrook* 59

Loving the Land in Lynden, *Ron Polinder* 75

An Urban Future, *Aimee Frazier* 93

Voluntary Conservation, *Dean Kahn* 109

Whatcom Place Names, *Robert Keller* 129

The Whatcom Land Trust recognizes that people arrive at conservation decisions through diverse paths; therefore we have encouraged the authors in this book to draw upon individual experience and to express their personal convictions.

Second Edition
©2006 Whatcom Land Trust
ISBN 0–9657053–3–1
ISBN 978–0–9657053–3–2

A Sacred Place

William Dietrich

"I walked…and stopped to look in awe at sunlight filtering through trees…" *Sybil Sanford, artist*

Photo: Helen Scholtz

Anthropologists tell us that one of the earliest and most universal religious ideas is the sacred place. It might be a druidic gnarled oak in England, or a cedar grove honored by the Lummi Indians in the shadowy Nooksack Valley. It might be a mountain top like Zion, center of Jerusalem: by legend the spot where Abraham was prepared to sacrifice Isaac, and where Mohammed later ascended for a tour of Heaven. Or it might be Mount Baker, Komo Kulshan. It could be as specific as Stonehenge or as general as the Dakota Black Hills. The Mongols had a peak, Burkhan Khaldun, that was center of the world to Genghis Khan. The Greeks had Olympus and Delphi.

We in Northwest Washington, the "Fourth Corner" of the United States, are blessed to live in such a place. It is one of those geographies so beautiful, so moody, so varied, and so powerful that it serves as a gate, a station platform, for the spiritual. It confirms our suspicion that there is more to life than everyday survival. It reenforces our hunch that there is a reality deeper than what we commonly see. This has nothing to do with religious dogma. It has everything to do with finding meaning beyond materialism, and serenity beyond sensation. Our land and sea, from the scattered emeralds of the San Juan Islands to the crystal crest of the Cascades, is surely a place where gods dwell, pixies cavort, mermaids swim, and trolls brood under piles of mossy boulders. Bald eagles have anointed it. Herons stand sentry. To conserve and protect such a place is a spiritual act. To destroy it is desecration.

Ancient Egyptians believed words and names were so powerful that they were magic, and I hope we retain that reverence. The

Whatcom Land Trust relies on community support for its preservation of imperiled places, and its word "trust" not only implies that we trust the organization to hold and protect our heartland for future generations, but that it trusts us to sustain its mission. This book is a means to do so. It is a communion, if you will, between its contributors and its readers—a commemoration of a landscape that, in its richness and ability to inspire, is holy.

Egyptian temples had a series of gates and doorways leading from chamber to chamber, to places ever more intimate, dim, and sacred. I think of Northwest Washington in much the same way. Interstate 5's Conway Hill, which first reveals the panorama of the Skagit Valley, is like an entry causeway. The Chuckanut Highlands is a castle portcullis leading to a Bellingham that has the potential to be beatific. From the water, Deception Pass, Guemes Channel, or the inlets flanking the southern fortress wall of Lummi Island give the same sense of entry. Beyond, Baker and its valleys beckon. The feeling continues as one explores eastward past tulip fields and raspberry farms to the maple and alder corridors of the Nooksack and Skagit, canyons narrowing, climbing upward, each glimpse east revealing sharper and more dazzling peaks. Eventually we reach that wonderland of glacier and wildflower meadow that surely is a template of heaven. Whatcom. A cornucopia of ecosystems! There is tidal marsh, diked pasture, nested lakes, plunging falls, Ent-like old growth, scarlet huckleberries, and mountain scree. Species number in the thousands, and trails invite a lifetime of exploration. What we lack in fabled dragons we more than make up in secretive Bigfoot and elusive grizzlies. How privileged we are! And with privilege comes responsibility.

One pioneer who crossed a low shoulder of Mount Baker while traveling north from the Skagit heard an odd primeval grinding as he descended to the silver Nooksack. The sound was mysterious, disturbing, like a rumbling factory in the middle of a wilderness. Reaching the Nooksack's edge, he discovered the sound was not some human machine, nor snoring monster, but rather that of spawning salmon, hundreds of thousands of them, digging nests in the river gravel. That's what we've lost in less than a hundred and fifty years: that astonishing sound of regeneration. Our civilization is cocky and quick, but has yet to prove it can sustain itself.

We live in migratory times. Careers flicker with change. Technology is breathless. Friendships can be as momentary as flash powder. Experiences are pasted like stamp collections. It's exciting, but hollowing. We need a center, an anchor. Increasingly, that anchor is place. From landscape we draw identity, continuity, and balance. Preservation is not luxury; it's as fundamental to human health as eating. GNP in the Fourth Corner stands for glorious natural product, and we've all had days here when we feel richer than Croesus.

Go, visit what you see in these pages. Then pass your inheritance to generations yet to come.

William Dietrich grew up near Puget Sound in the shadow of Mount Rainier. His Pulitzer-winning non-fiction has been widely used in university classes. His fiction has been translated into eight languages.

Whatcom County enjoys rich and fertile soil in a rough
and rugged landscape.
Photo: Jon Brunk

Whatcom Places

Robert Keller

"The most telling sign of old age is not caring anymore."

Anonymous

Located between Seattle and Vancouver, B.C., Whatcom County, with its relatively small 170,000 population, offers a respite from the strain and stress of large cities. Its 143 miles of saltwater beaches and 3,000 miles of rivers and streams, its proximity to the San Juan Islands, and its backdrop of Cascade peaks make Whatcom County a place cherished by residents and envied by visitors. This book, first and foremost, celebrates that landscape.

Beaches, lakes, mountains, islands and open space also encourage future growth and development. While rising population brings certain advantages, it also means changes in land use: some rural lands have become urban or suburban; open space is more limited; agricultural land will transform into residential sites; low elevation forests can retreat and shrink; natural vistas of surface and sea increasingly become scenes of human occupation and activity. We ask you to consider the challenges of such change.

Old-timers and newcomers alike, whatever their politics or economic status, agree that Whatcom County today is an attractive place to live. Resort advertising speaks of "unspoiled shorelines…land left much as Nature created it…

Trees dating back ten centuries stand above Canyon Lake Community Forest.
Photo: Gordon Scott

Robert Keller, a board member of Whatcom Land Trust, is Professor Emeritus in History from Western Washington University.

February clouds serve as a dramatic backdrop to Eliza
Rock and Eliza Island as seen from Samish Crest.
Photo: Kevin Kelliher

architecture that respects and blends with the pristine beauty of this dazzling region."

Almost everyone agrees on what they like: it's not only jobs and a healthy economy, but the setting, public safety, quiet nights, fertile soil, clean air and water, easy access to trails and boating. Almost everyone wants to retain these treasures—but there is no consensus on how to do so. As is evident from the various voices in this book, people view Whatcom County from many perspectives, some compatible, some not. "Love for the earth," a Montana rancher has written, "is not exclusive to any class, occupation, or political persuasion." Facing our future thus requires an ongoing dialogue in public forums that include government, business, churches, special interests, commissions, the media. For some, there is also the forum of doing nothing. We address none of these venues here, except the last. Waiting and doing nothing is unacceptable if we hope to protect our heritage.

Whatcom Places advocates a particular type of action: the voluntary care of land by citizen groups, by business, and by landowners. A Land Trust member has succinctly defined stewardship as the responsibility of private landowners to care for their land. Aldo Leopold, the 20th century's premier ecological writer, expressed the same idea:

> *…that land is a community is the basic concept of ecology, but that land is to be loved and respected is an extension of ethics…. Land is not merely soil; it is a fountain of energy flowing through a circuit of soils, plants and animals…whoever owns land*

The view from the eastern boundary of Whatcom County encompasses the Pasayten Wilderness, North Cascades National Park, Jack Mountain, Hozomeen Mountain, the Ross Lake National Recreation Area and Whatcom Pass, with Mount Shuksan and Mount Baker in the distance.

Photo: Grant Myers

The Nooksack River flows north below Sumas Mountain, west
past Everson and Lynden, then turns south through Ferndale
and Lummi Indian lands.

Photo: Grant Myers

How we see Whatcom County depends on perspective.
Here the Nooksack River flows from Komo Kulshan,
"the Great White Watcher," spilling into a plain near
Deming and Nugent's Corner.

Photo: Manuel Rod del Pozo

The Nooksack River carries huge loads of eroded sand and silt from the mountains and deposits them at its delta in Bellingham Bay.

Photo: Tore Ofteness

has assumed, whether he knows it or not, the divine functions of creating and destroying.

A Sand County Almanac (1948)

For Americans, part of our strong social fabric has always been voluntary ethical action by concerned citizens. When writing *Democracy in America* more than 170 years ago, Alexis de Tocqueville observed that this "most democratic country on the face of the earth" was one in which its members eagerly joined together, outside of government and outside of their work, to promote and protect their common values. "Nothing," he informed Europeans in 1835, "is more deserving of our attention than the moral associations of America." We have maintained this tradition of voluntary civic responsibility through the Kiwanis and Rotary, through churches, garden clubs, civil rights groups, battered women's shelters, hiking organizations, nature advocacy groups, and numerous other associations. It is a crucial way of being patriotic.

Regard for this particular land, Whatcom County, can unite us to act beyond our own immediate self-interests, beyond our own temporary occupations. *Whatcom Places* honors beauty of landscape, fertility of soil, and the mystery of nature as seen by perceptive photographers; we hope they inspire a sense of belonging and respect for the land. The book acknowledges a few of the many caring people who have acted out of a generosity of spirit toward the future. And, finally, it seeks to capture a feeling for place—"if you don't know where you are, you don't know who you are"—and to convey the essence of patriotism, the love of one's homeland.

Point Roberts on Georgia Strait, part of Whatcom County, is cut off from Canada by a political quirk called the 49th parallel.
Photo: Tore Ofteness

Semiahmoo Bay and Spit was the site of a boom town during the Fraser River gold rush of 1858.
Photo: Tore Ofteness

Boaters glide past a tide pool at Larrabee State Park. In 1915, the Larrabee family donated 20 acres of land to the state, which became Washington's first state park. Today, the park covers 2,683 acres, with 8,100 feet of saltwater shoreline on Samish Bay, two lakes, and gorgeous sunsets.

Photo: Grant Myers

Shorelines

Dave Peebles

On an October morning I crunch through gravel at Larrabee Park's Wildcat Cove. A woman bundled against the chill perches on a drift log, watching her toddler splash fistfuls of gravel into the water. Nudging heaps of eel grass aside, a beachcomber stoops to look for an agate or puzzle over a crab's moulted husk. I slide the kayak off my shoulder and onto the water, drop into the cockpit and snap the sprayskirt around the coaming. I lean on the paddle and turn into open water.

A few brisk strokes bring me to rocks that lie a hundred yards offshore. From the west, a bruise of high cirrus spreads across the sky like an omen. The pale sun already casts a watery eye, anemic rays leaking through autumn's vapor-laden air. The warm-up uncongeals my blood.

At this stage of tide the kayak slips over a small shoal between rocky outcroppings whose untold generations of crumbled shells have built a white beach. These rocks once joined the sandstone cliff, though imagination must stretch further to envision ancient processes that separated the rocks from the point, or formed the point itself.

As I turn northward, cabins as well as substantial homes dot the cliffs beyond the cove. The eye slides over most of these as unobtrusive details in a dramatic shorescape. Here and there a canoe or skiff lies across drift logs. A couple in an old plywood rowboat

Inland marine waters support complex ecological relationships among diverse life forms such as this kelp crab (*Pugettia producta*) preparing to molt in a tide pool at Larrabee State Park.
Photo: Mark Turner

Dave Peebles taught at Sehome High School for 25 years and is active in the Washington Water Trails Association.

back up toward a buoy, the woman maneuvers with the oars while the man twists around to raise a crabpot.

A quarter-mile further north, Whiskey Rock reveals its former connection with Governors Point, a reef that lies exposed and unpassable at low water. Today the kayak crosses with room to spare, threading between barnacle-encrusted boulders. I watch for turnstones and harlequin ducks that favor such reefs for winter foraging. An occasional eagle surveys the scene imperiously. Great blue herons, ubiquitous on Whatcom County coastlines, leapfrog along the shore until they tire of the game and circle around behind the advancing kayak. A seal pops up now and again, obsidian eyes like black portals into the void. An otter family at times will cavort here in boisterous waves, but today attend to other business.

The surge lifts me as gently as the breathing of a comatose giant. Pausing to dwell on fantastic formations of sandstone cliff, I drift in close, press my palms against a sheer face or overhanging ledge, and scrutinize shapes and textures. My awareness turns to tectonic forces rumbling deep beneath the hull, forces that thrust up Chuckanut sandstone for an interface with the sea.

Everywhere sea and land embrace. Shore configuration and bottom contours shape wave and current, which in turn sculpt the shore. Winter storms out of the southeast, or brisk northwest winds and "smoky southwesters" spilling out of summer's high pressure, hurl waves at Governors and Clark's points. These rebound sharply, then vanish in an instant as they meet the incoming sea.

Waves shape any shoreline throughout eons of sheer relentless hammering, but something about these cliffs

The *ARCO Anchorage* passes Lummi Island en route to Cherry Point.
Photo: Tore Ofteness

The new Taylor Avenue boardwalk north of Fairhaven has quickly become a popular destination for walkers, runners and view-lovers.
Photo: Manuel Rod del Pozo

The view from Marine Drive on the north shore of Bellingham Bay
offers vistas of Bellingham, Fairhaven and Chuckanut Mountain.

Photo: Brett Baunton

Dunlins (*Calidris alpina*), a medium-size sandpiper, cluster on the sandstone shoreline at Larrabee State Park.

Photo: Gene Davis

defies obvious explanation. The sandstone artwork that brackets Chuckanut Bay lies not where water presently meets stone but five to 15 feet above high tide, the work of a sculptor whose dreams seem delicate, almost ethereal, not cataclysmic.

Mesmerized by this mystery, I count links back down the geologic chain. Prior to sculpting at different sea levels (a process ongoing even now, though at an imperceptible pace), before these beds uplifted and tilted, strata of sand punctuated by gravel beds were laid down in a basin or lake. Plant fossils show that Chuckanut sandstones were of freshwater or brackish origin. A windstorm, flood, or landslide buried various plants; perhaps they logjammed in the twist of a creek or sunk into the ooze of a bog.

Some beds accumulated sand, silt, and gravel to thousands and even tens of thousands of feet. Such layers in turn were uplifted and folded by the very tectonic forces that fret and dream in fitful slumber under our homes and malls and highways. But geology's earthscope can probe even further, producing a time-lapse movie reaching back beyond the building and eroding of mountain ranges to show a supercontinent breaking up, spinning off our North American fragment to embark on its own continuing westward trajectory across the face of the globe.

Shoreline paddling opens a window to the sea bottom. Deep purple sea stars and a scattering of their pale-orange morphs propagate along this rocky coast, as well as sea urchins and the occasional sea cucumber. Tiny pipe fish, related to sea horses, flutter like green ribbons, perfectly camouflaged by eel grass. Minuscule

George Garlick, a volunteer land steward for The Nature Conservancy, often checked Chuckanut Island, near his home on Pleasant Bay. A defender of nature, he died in 2005 at the age of 93.

Photo: Charles Nishida–Courtesy of The Nature Conservancy

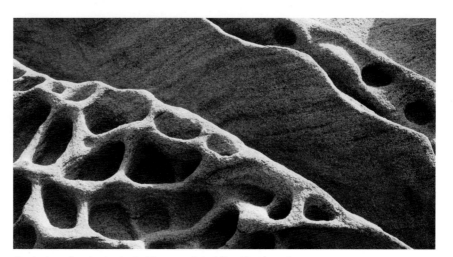

Centuries of water and wind have sculpted the Chuckanut sandstone cliffs at Larrabee State Park and Clayton Beach south of Bellingham.

Photo: Mark Turner

Guests are welcome at the annual Lummi Indian Stommish
celebration in June. The event features canoe races among
tribes from British Columbia and Washington.

Photo: Sharon Eva Grainger

Darrell Hillaire, Lummi
Photo: Manuel Rod del Pozo

The dorsal fin of a resident orca (*Orcinus orca*) provides an elegant and recognizable marker for whale watchers.

Photo: Patrick Reeves

The land and the waters of Whatcom County are part of my ancestors' homeland, a homeland that extends from the farthest island in the San Juans out to the mountains. Within the land and the water lie the teachings for how we should live our lives within the Lummi Reservation, within Whatcom County, and within our entire homeland. The land and water possess a spiritual life that is shared with our people. I believe in that spiritual life. I believe it is sacred.

Our elders taught me to respect nature, that if you take care of nature, nature will take care of you.

For me, the cedar tree is special because my mate is a basket maker. She makes things for friends from cedar and she encourages them to enjoy what she makes and not let baskets sit on a shelf.

The salmon is always present in our community. They are the miner's canary for our people: as the salmon goes, so go our people.

All living things have a place in our art and in our storytelling. We have much to learn. As an elder once said, "After all, humans are the youngest of all living things."

Darrell Hillaire

barnacles indicate high tide, the topmost fringe almost pioneers of air; a little lower, their large relatives cluster in rockscape cities. Bladderweed drapes the barnacles at mid-tide and, deeper yet, broad-leaved seaweeds of midnight purple shimmer with iridescence as if smeared with oil. Kelp crabs graze the canopy of this aquatic grove. I search pocket beaches and shallow coves for Dungeness crabs lurking in eel grass.

Beyond Clark's Point toward Bellingham I read a different story in a more recent chapter. Just south of Fairhaven, the sandstone gives way to glacial deposits and alluvial benches. From here northward, our bays and coves are broad and shallow. Driven seas stumble across shoal bottoms and break into surf. Some bays become mudflats at low tide—poor timing at Drayton Harbor can strand the paddler in a morass of pungent, boot-sucking mud.

Rivers and streams partly account for the shallow Whatcom County bays. Chuckanut Creek infills behind BNSF Railway's causeway. During heavy runoff the Nooksack River and Whatcom, Squalicum, and Little Squalicum creeks roil Bellingham Bay with sediments. Unwary sailors have run aground nearly a mile off the Nooksack delta. Lummi Bay, a broad mudflat at low tide, is an offspring of the Lummi River, principal outlet of the Nooksack River only a century ago. Terrell Creek contributes sediment to Birch Bay, while Dakota and California creeks help clog Drayton Harbor. For places like these, slow death is inevitable.

Near Squalicum, unmistakable signs of glacial deposition appear. The putty-colored bluffs along Eldridge Avenue, behind Little Squalicum Beach, and as far west

Alaska ferries dock regularly at Fairhaven, the southern terminus of Alaska's state ferry system.
Photo: Marcy Bloomenthal

Boulevard Park is part of a Greenways effort to protect a nature corridor along the marine bluff south of downtown Bellingham.
Photo: Courtesy of the Port of Bellingham

Local writer Tom Robbins once wrote of Pacific Northwest skies:
"...and the sun is a little boiled potato in a sea of dirty dumplings."
Photo: Sharon Eva Grainger

Water defines, enhances, and sustains life.
Photo: Sharon Eva Grainger

as Cliffside Drive are glacial till and outwash. These promontories of clay, sand, gravel, and boulders erode inexorably into Sir William Bellingham's bay, augmenting the work of rivers and creeks. Portage Island's Point Frances, as well as bluffs along Cherry Point, Point Whitehorn, Birch Point and Point Roberts, are similar, laid down by glaciers dating back 30,000 years and ending a mere 12,000 years ago.

A sudden swirl alerts the paddler along these points to submerged "erratics," granite monsters transported south from the Canadian coastal range on the backs of glaciers. Currents carry sediment from the eroding points to build spits at Semiahmoo and Sandy Point.

Glaciers acquire their burden by grinding down landscape. Whatcom County shorelines testify to this as well. Off the western side of Lummi Island, Lummi Rocks bear a glacier's unmistakable imprint of long, parallel grooves inscribed into rock. I can trace them with a paddle from the kayak, or scramble onto rocks to reach other scars dozens of yards long, left by a juggernaut that engulfed the entire inland sea from the Cascades to Vancouver Island and the Olympics, overtopping not only Lummi Mountain, but Mount Constitution on Orcas as well.

Paddlers poking along Whatcom County bays encounter still another shaper of landscape, one whose urge to bend the world to his own ends has left significant, though scarcely eternal, marks. Within one short century, many piers, canneries, log dumps, and railheads have vanished, except for scattered rotted pilings and twisted tracks. Tumbled slabs of broken concrete,

Dunlins are handsome, approachable, and hardy.
Photo: Fredrick Sears

Patterns in Chuckanut sandstone are often beautiful, sometimes startling, and sometimes puzzling.
Photo: Gene Davis

A county park at Teddy Bear Cove, acquired through Whatcom Land Trust, provides access to the saltwater wonders of Chuckanut Bay. Whatcom Land Trust holds a conservation easement to ensure protection of the beach and the Douglas-fir slope above it.

Photo: Manuel Rod del Pozo

Portage and Lummi islands provide the backdrop for this view from Lummi Shore Drive.

Photo: Manuel Rod del Pozo

Lummi Basket

With Fran's and Anna's
help, I wove a basket.
Beneath my fingers
cedar bark and raffia
entwined a Lummi past
and I exclaimed my joy.
Before my eyes, a design
of your tradition became
woven into my life.

Do I astonish you when
I fill this basket
with my praise?
It is the basket which
I marvel at. It is being
present to its making
while you talk over
family matters
that brings my happiness
to overflowing.

In its center
a piece of beargrass
circles round in mine,
like yours, across the table.
No matter where I look
I find your pattern
woven into mine.
This is a gift
between us.

Carla Shafer, Bellingham

Reef-netters bring in a haul at Lummi Island's Legoe Bay.
Photo: Manuel Rod del Pozo

rusted iron, a jagged "rock" of zinc below Chrysalis Inn, and shards of brick—artifacts of human endeavors already faded from memory—form the "beaches" of Boulevard Park and outside Mount Baker Products. Detritus we once hoped to forget bubbles up from the landfill beyond lower Cornwall Avenue, itself the result of dredge spoils dumped to reclaim a mudflat. The partially demolished Georgia-Pacific mill site sits quietly, awaiting decisions about what will rise there, how its stretch of industrial waterfront will be revised for shops, businesses, parks, and homes.

Threading between log booms in Whatcom Creek waterway, I try not to spook sunbathing seals or sea lions draped over logs. From here I measure my kayak against oceangoing tugs, watching from a safe distance as these little goliaths dodge and pirouette to nudge freighters into piers. When an idle crew member waves, I lift my paddle.

After snooping into the dank underworld beneath docks, I detour through Squalicum Harbor. Sailboats scurry out for an evening race, cruisers lay a course for the islands, purse seiners rumble by to stalk salmon. Kayaks co-exist easily with gillnetters, but must be more cautious riding a flood between the reef gear deployed in Legoe Bay. Near the shoals of Portage Island, Lummi Indians stretch nets from the shore, and approaching Gooseberry Point I can dart behind the tiny ferry that shuttles islanders to and from their homes.

Bellingham strollers can catch a glimpse of this world from the Taylor Avenue dock and boardwalk. And in September 2006, thanks to Trillium Corporation,

Reef-net technology at Lummi Island was developed by native
people before European contact.

Photo: Sharon Eva Grainger

Fishing boats unload their salmon catch on Bellingham's waterfront. Salmon fishing was once a major industry in the Northwest, with Bellingham the home of Pacific American Fisheries, the largest Pacific salmon cannery in the world. Overfishing and diminished habitat have greatly reduced commercial fishing in the Northwest, but it remains an iconic activity that warrants preservation and enhancement.

Photo: Brett Baunton

Whatcom County Parks and Recreation Department and Whatcom Land Trust, sea lovers gained a long stretch of public beach south of Point Whitehorn.

When I visit the still-wild parts of Whatcom County's shoreline, my first impulse is to think "timeless." Yet abundant evidence contradicts that delusion. Throughout our stretch of coast, each place is caught in some particular moment and sign of transformation: cracks in cliffs that delineate future seastacks; hollows and honeycombs that are a mere gleam in the sculptor's eye; shattered sandstone eggshells that perhaps hatched behemoths a day before yesterday; silt-choked bays, moribund or already dead, whose rivers and creeks unburden cargoes of sand, the mud-mountains already piling up compound interest in sedimentary savings accounts; future sandstones prepared to uplift and wear down.

Our shoreline, together with all that mighty Cascadian upland that backs it, is but a grace note in the vast cosmic symphony—itself a work in progress. We, in our brief foray, dream that we possess it and mold it to our will. But we are at best transient stewards, often mere pillagers or interlopers, ever evanescent shadows…stardust.

Witness

The morning is mothy with fog.
the outer shore cannot be seen.
the window sweats for more heat.
The only moving is someone walking
the inner shore the tide has changed…

Kenneth E. Warfel, Bellingham

The monument at Zuanich Point Park in Bellingham honors Whatcom County fishers who went to sea, never to return.
Photo: Brett Baunton

Five-acre Chuckanut Island is owned by the Nature Conservancy. Its western cove is a popular landfall for kayaks and canoes.

Photo: Gene Davis

Clyde Ford, author

Photo: Manuel Rod del Pozo

A resident harbor seal *(Phoca vitulina)* basks in the sun. Seals, cherished by most local citizens, are the only year-round resident marine mammals left in Whatcom County waters.

Photo: Patrick Reeves

Water was a big reason I came here and certainly one of the reasons I've stayed. I'd been a kayaker for just two or three months and was out in Wildcat Cove where two gray whales played with us in the kayak, circling, diving under the boat—it was so miraculous. Since then I've also been in a pod of orcas. You just let go, allowing a force much greater than yourself to be in control.

Here, water is accepted as an important element, if not sacred, a meaningful aspect of where we live.

On the sea we gain a different view of the horizon, a dividing line between what we know and don't know. The horizon symbolizes adventure and a presence of the unknown. On the sea, that's ever present. At the same time, at sea we have this sense of the Earth being one unified place. The sea has personality, and it changes. On land we experience seasons, but on the sea change is not seasonal, it's daily, with currents and tides constantly shifting beneath us.

A sense of place has strong meaning for me, for most people. Some places call me and I feel most at home there. From Bellingham to northern British Columbia, out in our boat or kayak, I truly feel at home even though I grew up in New York City. My concern is that development not obliterate this sense of place I've connected to in Whatcom County.

Traditional societies had mythologies of place, which would sanctify where they lived, not only physically but spiritually. Ability to relate to a place that way, the sense of being connected spiritually with land, that's incredibly important. You feel the place physically and you feel it psychically, a spiritual geography of meaning.

At sea you're always looking toward land for safe harbor. In some ways, that's symbolic of our lives: "Where's the next safe harbor?"

Clyde Ford

Hozomeen Mountain (8,080') rises east of the Skagit River just south of the Canadian border. The north peak was first climbed by a U.S. Topographic Survey crew and the south peak in 1947 by Fred Becky. Writer Jack Kerouac once manned the fire lookout in the foreground on nearby Desolation Peak.

Photo: John Scurlock

Rugged and Roadless

Wendy Walker

Beyond Mount Baker, Whatcom County crumples upward into an engineer's nightmare of jagged peaks and deeply gouged canyons. Such terrain comprises more than half the county, stretching eastward 50 miles to a boundary in the Pasayten Wilderness called the Cascade Crest Trail.

Humans have yet to subdue this wild landscape. No roads penetrate the heart of the mountains, the only structures being fire lookouts and a few old mining cabins. The east remains a wilderness sanctuary, a thousand-square-mile undeveloped place that separates the towns and farms of the west from sparsely settled ranching and orchard country in the Okanogan.

Eastern Whatcom County retains the character of a place newly born after millennia of glaciation. When mountains emerged from melting continental ice 10,000 years ago, bare rock provided an opening for new life to spin its web. Many of today's plants and animals belong to these pioneering young ecosystems. Alpine glaciers still carve the spires and ridges of the highest peaks. Meltwater streams cascade into primeval valleys thick with conifer forests that endure and even thrive despite 30 feet of winter snow, a two-month growing season, torrential rains and long droughts.

For much of the year, snow smothers this eastern half. Some places never lose their cold blanket, a glacial reminder that ice ages

The mountain wildlife community is known for its distinctive characters: the whistling marmot, squeaking pika, majestic mountain goats and here, a ptarmigan (*Lagopus leucurus*) who relies on plumage as the best defense.
Photo: Grant Myers

Wendy Walker lives in Blaine and is a professor at Huxley College, Western Washington University.

Artist Point, at the eastern end of the Mount Baker Highway,
provides breathtaking views of Mount Shuksan (above) and
Mount Baker.

Photo: Grant Myers

A climber approaching the summit of Mount Baker (10,778') peers into steaming Sherman Crater. Mt. Baker is an active volcano.

Photo: Brett Baunton

For some, new forms of mountain recreation are more exhilarating than scaling peaks. Mount Baker has an active snowboading community, with competitive events such as the Legendary Banked Slalom.

Photo: Patrick Reeves

Climbers peer into a glacial crevasse on Mount Challenger south of Whatcom Pass.

Photo: Bob and Ira Spring

The first Ski to Sea race, aka Mount Baker Marathon, began at 10:00 a.m., Thursday, August 10, 1911. The annual event continues today.

Photo: Jon Brunk

do return. Few humans venture long into the wild country during winter's frigid temperatures and thunderous avalanches.

In the spring, as snow melts, the land softens and wakens to rushing streams and budding leaves. The short summer is halcyon and unrestrained as blooming wildflowers, clouds of insects and flocks of birds fill mountain meadows and forests. For a month or two, the high country becomes hospitable to mountain goats, marmots and humans.

Autumn's chill, sunny days bring vibrant reds and oranges. Blueberries ripen. Eagles, hawks and jays migrate south. Mammals hibernate or move to lower elevations as October winds bring early sleet and snow. Eastern Whatcom returns to its isolation.

Black bear, cougar and wolverine still inhabit these mountains through the cycle of seasons. A few grizzly may survive. Wolves are returning to the Cascades from Canada and wild salmon still spawn here. There may be animals in eastern Whatcom County that have never sensed a human, whose whole universe remains undisturbed by civilization.

Mountains that defy roadbuilding are an outdoor enthusiast's dream. Hikers enjoy a thousand or more trail miles; climbers scale peaks ringed by ice; kayakers, canoeists, and rafters run untamed rivers. It's possible to live for weeks remote from any road. But our wildlands are more than playground. They offer renewal, mental and spiritual balance, a chance to rediscover challenges of living simply amid wilderness rhythms, the euphoria of knowing something more powerful and more profound than human affairs.

High alpine ridge walks call to backpackers in the Mount Baker
Wilderness Area.

Photo: Brett Baunton

Whatcom County travelers have discovered images of Mount Shuksan (9,127')
from Picture Lake—considered the most photographed view in the world—
in Africa, India, Israel, Germany, and the Swiss Alps.
Photo: Mark Bergsma

Sibyl Sanford, artist
Photo: Manuel Rod del Pozo

Autumn Mist (detail)
Watercolor: Sibyl Sanford

I started with watercolors as a little girl, painting Maine landscapes with my father, who was my first art teacher. We'd sit on rocks at the beach and paint. We had a wonderful relationship, the beginning of my love of watercolors and for nature.

In 1971, I arrived from Colby College in Maine to work in the North Cascades with the Student Conservation Corps. I just fell in love with this land, its mountains, the wild places. I returned after graduation to work for the Forest Service, where I met Wendy Walker. The two of us worked as rangers in the Glacier Peak Wilderness. That's when I decided to spend my life in the Pacific Northwest, which became the inspiration for painting.

Watercolor suits me well. It's a meditative, peaceful, lovely medium. When I paint nature I focus on emotions springing up inside me. Working in my studio, I hear sounds that I heard outdoors, smell the smells, feel a sense of place. I hope it comes through, that love of the moment, expressing the invisible spirit of outdoors. It's more about what you don't see than what you do see.

I walked in Arroyo Park yesterday and stopped to look in awe at sunlight filtering through trees. I just stood still for minutes. Art has developed in me an appreciation of small things—how light hits objects, green leaves against a muted background, designs on a rock, tiny bits of moss. Wild land is sacred ground. At Chuckanut, Arroyo, Fragrance Lake, Mount Baker, and all the trails, enjoying mountain streams as well as the sea, I find such peace, observing and feeling close to creatures and plants. It's immensely healing.

Sibyl Sanford

Imagine...descending into brooding old growth, lying beneath a 1,000-year-old cedar, looking upward through gnarled branches at blue sky...strolling an alpine meadow alive with butterflies and blossoms, sweet scents swirling in a summer breeze...climbing sheer rock faces and finally standing exhilarated on the wind-blasted summit with a maze of crags in all directions. These too are Whatcom places.

Such natural areas sustain those of us who live and work in the western half. Mountains, among other things, determine weather, supply water and assist with waste removal; they contribute to air quality, hydropower, soil, biodiversity, pharmaceutical research, and global climates. The Cascades create weather by snagging Pacific storms: huge masses of wet clouds roll in, slam into a barrier, rise, cool, and dump most of their moisture, much in the form of snow, on the western slopes. Accumulating during winter, melting during summer, glaciers and snowpack become reservoirs to sustain lakes, streams, and people.

Early white explorers got it right when they called these mountains the Cascades. Waterfalls tumble down almost every cliff. Streams gurgle in almost every valley. It's hard to find a silent place in the North Cascades; water roars, crashes or trickles almost everywhere.

The Nooksack and Skagit rivers collect their tributaries and head west and south, fluid transportation networks that bring drinking water and irrigation to numerous small towns. A minor diversion extracts power at Nooksack Falls. Three dams and a powerhouse—Ross, Diablo, Gorge, Newhalem—on Whatcom's portion of

Is all the exertion and effort worth it? Hikers and climbers in the North Cascades answer with a resounding "yes!"
Photo: Steve Satushek

Nooksack Cirque outflow from Mount Shuksan joins other streams below
Hannegan Pass to create Whatcom County's major river, the Nooksack.

Photo: Marcy Bloomenthal

The Nooksack, fed by snow and glacier-melt from the mountains, maintains a steady year-round flow.

Photos: Brett Baunton

A Branch for Winter

Walking along the Middle Fork of the Nooksack
There is a branch
you never noticed before,
even though you've walked
this trail your whole life. It hangs over the river
bearing heaviness of snow,
dipping once in awhile
to feel the currents pull. You remember times when
people seemed close,
when mornings made the world
around indifferent to what you thought mattered.
Now their voices follow your thoughts
through a mesh of hanging moss,
they will not leave—this is the way a friend should be
on a day that asks,
"Who will remember you?"

Matthew Campbell Roberts, Bellingham

The Twin Sisters seen from the east at Canyon Lake ridge provide an unfamiliar sight for most Whatcom County residents.
Photo: Roger Weiss

Trails into Whatcom County's high country above Ross Lake are reached mainly from Highway 20 via Skagit County and Newhalem.
Photo: Bob and Ira Spring

49

Diablo dam supplies one of four Seattle City Light powerhouses within Whatcom County.

Photo: Mark Turner

The North Cascades Institute's retreat and outdoor learning center on Diablo Lake boasts remarkable architecture in a spectacular setting.

Photo: Courtesy of North Cascades Institute

Ross Lake, which extends over 30 miles from Ross Dam to British Columbia, can be subject to sudden winds that make for dangerous paddling.

Photo: Jon Brunk

Glacial till, or "milk," creates an emerald view for motorists at the Diablo reservoir overlook on Highway 20, with Colonial Peak in the background.

Photo: Brett Baunton

Golden larch stand by an alpine lake on the eastern edge of
Whatcom County.

Photo: Brett Baunton

the Skagit account for much of Seattle's electricity. The Skagit below Newhalem remains free flowing; the Nooksack is almost entirely free of human restraint.

For Whatcom County, the Nooksack provides scant hydropower, yet we are rich beyond our wildest dreams, or as rich as our dreams of the wild. We live within several hours' drive of swift rivers, ancient forests and impossible peaks: Mount Baker Wilderness (122,000 acres), Noisy-Diobsud Wilderness (15,000 acres), North Cascades National Park (504,000 acres), Pasayten Wilderness (530,000 acres). It will require a long time for the Land Trust to acquire that much property. The wild, fortunately, is public. Each of us owns a share of:

- *hundreds of lakes*
- *millions of acres of forest*
- *countless streams and creeks*
- *an active volcano*
- *a thousand mountains*
- *hundreds of glaciers*

Every American shares this legacy, but we reside here. We are wealthy indeed.

With our riches comes special responsibility: to protect this heritage from abuse and from thoughtless human impact. We must invest in our future by being alert—acutely aware of the goals and actions of federal land managers and our local officials, men and women who will need our help in reaching decisions to protect these Whatcom places for centuries to come.

Mountains never teach apathy.

One of the most accessible and spectacular trails near Mount Baker follows Skyline Divide.
Photo: Steve Satushek

A popular hike for all ages is the Ptarmigan Ridge trail below Table Mountain near the Mount Baker ski area.
Photo: Steve Satushek

Less than 15 percent of Pacific Northwest ancient trees remain
standing, including these in the Mount Baker Wilderness Area.

Photo: Brett Baunton

A young red-shafted flicker (*Colaptes cafer*) greets his male parent.

Photo: Steve Satushek

Three loggers tackle a giant cedar in the era long before chainsaws.

Photo: Darius Kinsey, courtesy of the Whatcom Museum of History and Art

For much of the year, clouds blanket the timberline forests of
the North Cascades.

Photo: Tore Ofteness

Tom and Bonnie Westergreen, tree farmers

Photo: Manuel Rod del Pozo

Trillium *(Trillium ovatum)* is a distinctive woodland flower.

Photo: Helen Scholtz

Tom: My great grandfather Gust Westergreen came from Sweden when he was twenty, homesteading at the foot of Sumas Mountain in 1888. Trees and brush were cleared to farm, but most was left for cutting and growing trees. Grandpa Albert continued to farm and cut trees; he also purchased more land.

Just like his father, my dad, Richard, cleared some ground for cattle and bought additional cut-over land for growing trees. As kids, my two brothers and I helped Dad log or cut firewood. We planted trees, cut brush, built trails—anything to improve the property.

Our own tree farm has a timber goal, but because of its tree and plant diversity, we have more varieties of wildlife than in many protected areas. Right now we're doing more with cedar—saving natural saplings and planting new ones. We're starting to plant red alder, too.

Bonnie: You can barely tell where we've harvested because we replant and because we cut small sections, leaving huge trees elsewhere. It's a misconception that logging has to mean devastation and clear-cuts. What we have created is a very diverse forest.

Tom: My dad was involved in the beginning of the local chapter of the Washington Farm Forestry Association, which represents small forest landowners. The Association helps educate family tree farmers and keeps forest management a viable, sustainable endeavor. A tree farm brings a lot of benefits to the community: wildlife habitat, watershed protection, clean air, recreation, and renewable wood products. "He who plants trees loves others" reflects our feelings; a lot of what we do is for our grandchildren and their grandchildren.

Tom & Bonnie Westergreen

An opening in the foothills close to Saxon provides a glimpse
of the Twin Sisters near a divide between the Nooksack River's
south fork and the Samish River.

Photo: Lee Mann

Foothills

Binda Colebrook

Twenty miles east as the raven flies from the Strait of Georgia and Birch Bay, the northernmost Cascade foothills begin. This northeast area, which encompasses the towns of Sumas, Nooksack and northern Everson, lies in the Fraser River drainage. Here all water flows north via Sumas and Saar creeks, across the border and into our Canadian neighbor's domain.

Frequently the climate comes from the north. Hot, dry summer air flows out of the Canadian interior and overpowers the oceanic winds. In winter, freezing northeasters rage down the Fraser Canyon and into the valley, bringing snow, desiccation and a roaring as loud as a freight train. Dirt from cropless fields swirls in the air, giving a Gobi-esque quality to the scene.

Two northeast foothill sentinels, Vedder and Sumas mountains (the latter historically and more rightly called Nooksack Mountain), stand above the valley blocking winds, obscuring dawn and the eastern horizon, shining in the golden light of late afternoon and dominating the entire day with an endless play of color, mist, clouds, and vegetation. The two mountains are composites, scrapings off the oceanic plate: 65-million-year-old dinosaur-age sandstone; 100-million-year-old Mesozoic graywackes and shale; a scattering of 400-million-year-old limestone, chert, and shale; and a serpentine metamorphic of indeterminate age that was once part of the ocean floor. The foothills stand like islands in a sea of

Fifty years ago, few residents would have believed that wine-making would survive in Northwest Washington's cold, damp climate. This popular vineyard on the Mount Baker Highway comes alive every spring not only to survive, but to flourish.

Photo: Mark Bergsma

Binda Colebrook is an Everson writer and resident who specializes in native habitat restoration.

Salmon are an important food for bald eagles (*Haliaeetus leucoephalus*). Bird watchers can observe eagles by keeping a respectful distance from where salmon spawn and die.

Photo: Lee Mann

A unique wildlife conservation easement with the Trillium Corp. protects a bald eagle night roost at Kenney Creek on the Nooksack River near its middle fork.

Photo: Fredrick Sears

Snow and ice from Mount Baker and the North Cascades sustain the north fork of the Nooksack River.

Photo: Gordon Scott

"Who of us would not prefer to dwell on the ingenious disorder of a natural river landscape than on the trivial regularity of a straightened water course?"

Friedrich Schiller (1793)

Rain is much more frequent in Whatcom County than one might guess
from the images in this book. The sunlit drizzle in this scene near Potter
Road, South Fork Valley, is closer to reality.

Photo: Mark Turner

glacial outwash and recent alluviums. Barely 10,000 years ago, the most recent glaciers rose above the present town of Chilliwack, intermittently releasing their cargo of water-borne rocky debris out over the valleys of the Sumas and Nooksack rivers.

These outflows eroded long chains of wetlands that, in pre-settlement days, were filled with diverse native vegetation and huge noisy flocks of waterfowl so dense that local tribal people caught them by stringing nets between poles. In certain foothill pockets, large blocks of ice settled and depressed the land. That left kettle holes in which sphagnum moss and Labrador tea bushes grew and died for thousands of years, their acid layers creating a diary of changing pollen deposits and ash from volcanic eruptions.

Technically, Whatcom County is in the western hemlock/red cedar zone, but analysis of early surveys shows that about 37 percent of the land was periodically burnt over. The frequent fires created large patches of hazel and other shrubs scattered among dead trunks, young deciduous/conifer forests, and scrub-shrub wetlands. Where soil was too wet or too dry for trees, sedge meadows and grass prairies full of camas, Indian carrots and other flowers were maintained by the tribes. These fragile grasslands, a rare source of carbohydrates and medicinal plants, were quickly destroyed by plowing and by free-ranging frontier hogs.

In the middle drainage of the Sumas River, across the present British Columbia border, lay a great shallow lake, called Sumaahl, ten miles by eight, but nowhere deeper than 12 feet (Sumaahl means "big opening" in

Sumas Mountain rises above farmland between Deming and Everson, providing a scenic backdrop for this chapel at Nugent's Corner.
Photo: Brett Baunton

A coyote (*Canis latrans*) appears weary after chasing waterfowl.
Photo: Patrick Reeves

Whatcom Land Trust works to conserve family farms and the rich productivity of our agriculture, such as this hay field on Noon Road.

Photo: Jon Brunk

Trumpeter *(Cygnus buccinator)* and tundra *(Cygnus columbianus)* swans winter over in open farmland. The birds gain valuable sustenance from traditional crops.

Photo: Fredrick Sears

Mount Baker

When you grow up only on flatlands,
All those mountainous pictures look so Hollywood—
No mountains soar that steep,
Or are that milky white—
Touched up, brushed to glistening presentation,
Each is a towering ice cream sundae feast,
Cone turned upside down against blue sky.

Wheatland is a woven mat,
Ground level low, sight
Stretching straight over to horizons—
It is that flavorless flat,
Swept down, low, on a somber sea—
Never a glittering sundae
Dropped from the clouds with glee.

Seeing the mountain's tall whiteness
Come like a bolt from the blue
Has been a scene out of fancy—
One of those films from the '40s
Where children wake up astonished
To flowers turned sparkling gumdrops,
And amazing icy new snow.

The mountain's high peak doesn't stun us,
Every day that we glimpse up to see,
For woolly clouds snuggle around it,
Obscuring the magical scene—
But all of us searching for mountains,
Know that it's really marshmallow cream
Piled high on a rich sundae wonder,
In wait for eyes glinting great treats.

Llew Cheyenne, Bellingham

the Staalo's language.) Around its edge grew a large bluejoint prairie, where first the indigenous peoples and then Euro-American settlers wintered their horses and hunted grouse. Sumas Lake, which increased to 30,000 acres with spring freshets, was known for its "wapato," or Indian potatoes, a plant now almost extirpated from Whatcom County wetlands. It was one of the great sockeye, sturgeon (and mosquito) breeding grounds of the Fraser system.

The prairie was plowed and the lake drained in the 1920s, but the northwest face of Vedder Mountain still rises steeply from the valley floor. Those who hike or ride the logging roads gain marvelous views of the flat farmlands, Abbotsford, the trans-Canada highway, and the canyon of the Fraser as it heads east past Mount Cheam and then into a vast northern interior. Wild creatures as well as people use this corridor. Western kingbirds, Swainson's phoebes and meadowlarks wing through from the east. Flocks of swans, gulls and ducks feed in flooded winter fields, and cougar, bear, elk, deer, beaver, muskrat and otter still inhabit the forests and river edges. The great wolves are gone. Only the omnivorous coyote, which arrived in their absence and ate the smaller foxes, howl at the edge of farms and suburban home sites. Gone, too, are the huge salmon runs, that incredible quantity of protein that once fertilized the riparian areas and fed vultures, condors, eagles, crows and the many riparian mammals and invertebrates.

For thousands of years, ancestors of present-day Nooksack Indians occupied this area, harvesting protein

Once considered useful only for "reclaiming," today marsh lands, like those surrounding Lake Terrell, are valued for water retention and purification, waterfowl habitat, and a special calm beauty.

Photo: Gene Davis

From corn field to foothills to the Twin Sisters, many scenes in Whatcom County encompass both human endeavor and natural wonder.

Photo: Steve Satushek

Jonagold apples hang ripe in a Lynden orchard.
Photo: Margaretha Maryk

Moonlit Night

The breeze went through the fields,
The ears of grain surged softly,
The forests rustled gently,
The night was so star-bright.

And my soul extended
Its wings so wide,
It flew through the quiet regions
As though it were flying home.

Joseph von Eichendorf, 1788-1857

This farm near Everson sells more than 200 varieties of
fruiting plants.
Photo: Mark Turner

from watery habitats, the burnt-over brush and deep forests. They climbed ridges surrounding Mount Baker, seeking late-summer berries and hunting goats whose wool made prestigious blankets for ceremonial potlatches. To reinforce social ties and ensure resource sharing, they married with the Lummi to the west, the Staalo to the north in British Columbia, and the Skagit people to the south. Thus the large winter houses along the river edges heard bi- and trilingual conversations.

Today, dairies, produce farms and small industries inhabit the rich soil of the valley floor. On the lower foothills, traditional homestead families, loggers and farmers increasingly encounter many newcomers, retirees, vacationers and professionals. Second- and third-growth tree farms mix with clearcuts on private and state land. A few pockets of century-old forest survive, the large trunks and snags giving testimony to the past's immense cedars and Douglas-firs. Among them grow the now uncommon smaller species of the understory. But, in the main, the hills today are covered with alder, birch and maple woodlands—beautiful and welcoming, yet only a hint of Whatcom County's past, a landscape of memory.

A remnant of autumn lingers into winter on East Axton Road.
Photo: Steve Satushek

69

A juvenile kingfisher *(Ceryle alcyon)* perches, looking for fish.
Photo: Dick McNeely

Students from Kendall Elementary School stay dry while field
instructor Angileen Bates collects samples from Kendall Creek.
Photo: Courtesy of Nooksack Salmon Enhancement Association

Maple Creek flows from Silver Lake, drops over Maple Falls,
and enters the Nooksack River.
Photo: Grant Myers

The sun sets a grove aglow along the Nooksack River.
Photo: Helen Scholtz

Doug Huddle, hunter, fisherman

Photo: Manuel Rod del Pozo

Mountain lions (*Felis concolor*) are solitary, secretive hunters that feed on deer and smaller game.

Photo: Patrick Reeves

Whatcom County, over time, has lost some of the desirability it once had as a place to hunt and fish. Less and less land is available for hunters and fishers as we roll back habitat for hunted and non-hunted animals. "No Trespassing," "Keep Out," "No Hunting" signs are frequent. We had private places for decades where owners allowed, if not welcomed, hunting. New owners no longer welcome us.

I don't call anyone a hunter or fisherman if they commit disrespectful acts on somebody else's property, whether private, state or federal. People in the hunting fraternity have to respect land. And they must respect the game as well. Rules of fair chase don't permit animals to be chased down and shot from a vehicle or aircraft. These rules of the chase must be honored by hunters.

Today we've perhaps lost the visceral connection with our prey that aboriginal people had. The creature that you kill is a gift to you to sustain yourself, and must be appreciated in its own right. A hunter needs to understand his quarry, its habits, its tendencies. Serious hunters are good observers who pay attention to detail, fix images in their minds like little bits and pieces of a territorial jigsaw puzzle. Most hunters and fishermen tell me their primary experience is not the kill, it's being in a wild environment that requires heightened senses and speedy mental processing. Even if we don't get an animal, it's a good day to be alive in the outdoors.

Expert hunters hone skills of stalking, luring, observing, of camouflaging themselves, of moving carefully so not to disclose their presence. People who perfect these skills hearken back to when we hunted to survive and killed wild prey in order to have food.

Doug Huddle

Foothills carry a geologic and aesthetic message that rivals the highest peaks and glaciers.

Photo: Grant Myers

Our rich farm heritage provides self-sufficiency, a stable
economy, and aesthetic land uses.

Photo: Manuel Rod del Pozo

Loving the Land in Lynden

Ron Polinder

I grew up in the Lynden community. On second thought, I grew up when I moved away from Lynden. Not until my wife and I returned to rear our children, after nearly 20 years' absence, was I able to articulate how this place and people molded me.

As a lad I attended Lynden Christian School, where it was our custom to do a good bit of singing when the school day started. I now realize how songs from that old red songbook imprinted some foundational values. One was called "The Seed Song," No. 21. On the opposite page was placed the darkened silhouette of a farmer riding a sulky plow behind a team of horses. We sang:

See the farmer sow the seed while the field is brown;
See the furrows deep and straight up the field and down.
Wait a while and look again where the field was bare;
See how God has sent the corn growing golden there.
CHORUS: *Farmer, farmer, sow your seed up the field and down;*
God will make the golden corn grow where all is brown.

I liked the song, and the picture that went with it—they spoke to me.

Just what did the song say, one might ask? Simply put, it reminded me that God had a whole lot to do with what

Lynden's traditional Dutch culture is more than decor. It has its roots in religion and a land ethic.
Photo: Courtesy of the Port of Bellingham

Ron Polinder is former director of Concerned Christian Citizens and former principal of Lynden Christian High School.
In 2000, he became superintendent of Rehoboth Christian School, a century-old school primarily serving the Native American community in New Mexico.

happened on our family farm. Most of us who grew up near Lynden got the message, one way or another.

It may have come from the pastor's sermon, or the Prayer Day service, or the harvest dinner, but we learned that farming was a sacred activity not unlike going to church and school. All of life was related to religion. "Secular" was not a word in our vocabulary.

And so, the milk that poured into the tank, the oats that poured into the combine, the strawberry jam that poured into canning jars, were all pouring out of a blessing from the bounty of God's storehouse. We had been placed by God's good providence in a land of plenty. We lived along the river, the Nooksack, where soil was dark and rich. It is called "the river bottom" by locals, and we counted it a privilege to live there even though floods would occasionally put us to the test, and diking and ditching projects were an added expense.

But we also admired those farmers north of Lynden on a rich flat plain sprinkled with well-kept family farms. Berry farmers west of town were likewise honored. We would U-pick a few mornings every summer, marveling at the beauty of red, ripe berries. Mother would invariably chat with the owner or field boss, hoping they would find enough pickers to harvest the fruit and make a decent profit.

Lynden was a farming community. Townspeople realized that their livelihood was closely connected to the abundance that came from the earth. They went to Prayer Day services also, and made themselves available if you needed extra hands at haying time, or help bagging sand in flood season.

Agricultural land, Midwestern in tone and feel, adds to Whatcom County's variety. And here, as elsewhere, the transition from family farm to industrial agriculture tests a land ethic based on direct individual ownership.

Photo: Tore Ofteness

A Lynden plowing match occurs every April. Attention to
our heritage is also possible at various local museums, the
Peace Arch in Blaine, Berthusen Park in Lynden and Hovander
Homestead Park in Ferndale.

Photo: Mark Turner

Photo: Mark Turner

Whatcom County is a global power among raspberry producers, but also produces sizable crops of blueberries and strawberries.

Photo: Jason Glover, courtesy of Farm Friends

Photo: Brett Baunton

Life in Lynden in the '50s had a routine, a rhythm and a richness that offered a sense of security, identity and community. Mine was a privileged childhood, not because we were wealthy or free from problems, but because, comparatively speaking, we were secure. We knew who we were and from whence we had come. We were bound together by faith, family, and friends.

The '60s took many of us away, in my case away to far-off Calvin College in Grand Rapids, Michigan. The tumult of the '60s did not fully reach conservative colleges and small towns until the '70s, but revolutionary ideas were in the air and certainly under discussion in college classrooms. It was a marvelous decade to be a liberal arts student, to be exposed to the complexity of life and learning, to be challenged regarding the simple answers that accompany youthfulness. As a history major I learned that ideas have legs—they lead someplace. I began to understand the Enlightenment, the Age of Reason, the advance of science, technology, modernity. With it came the division of life into the sacred and the secular, that religion was to be privatized, that it should have little to do with politics, education or science. This rise of secularism was soundly critiqued; we came to see how it subtly subverted a theistic worldview and way of life.

Which brings us back home to Lynden and the agricultural community surrounding it. Has secularism overwhelmed the faith of the '50s where we started? As science and technology dramatically changed the face of farming, does it become easier to trust irrigation systems rather than prayer services? Have chemicals

Despite modern invention, many farms such as this one in north Whatcom County continue to rely on traditional hand-picking.

Photo: Steve Satushek, courtesy of Farm Friends

Whatcom County's fertile soil and temperate climate
have attracted dairy farmers from other parts of the country
and from other countries since the 1800s.

Photo: Jon Brunk, courtesy of Farm Friends

Shane VanderVeen, dairy farmer

Photo: Manuel Rod del Pozo

"… knowledge of place comes from working in it in all weathers, making a living from it, suffering its catastrophes, loving its mornings or evenings or hot noons, valuing it for the profound investment of labor that you, your parents and grandparents, your all but unknown ancestors, have put into it."

Wallace Stegner, *A Sense of Place*

We're milking 640 cows right now. We grow our own corn and silage. I enjoy it. I enjoy working with the cows, working the land, working with my family. That's a big thing. If I'm good to my animals, then they'll be good to me. Some cows are stubborn ones, cows that never seem to be in the right spot at the right time; you know their numbers and talk about them.

It's really essential to do a good job caring for the land, taking care of the water, no matter what the regulations say. I may not agree with all of them, but the idea of protecting the water, taking care of land, is important. Agriculture is important. Everyone needs food, and it creates open space.

Even big farms in Whatcom County have families running them. Dairy farms, berry farms, potato farms. It's a lifestyle, not just a job. It's not something that you can really put a price on. Because of this farm I observe things differently, like the weather.

Technology's also a major part of farming. All our cows now wear ankle bracelets linked to a computer that records how much each animal walks. We can tell if the cow is sick, active, or in heat. Does she need vet work, or hoof trimming? Every milking is recorded. With two low milk weights in a row, she might have a mastitis problem to take care of. As for our tractors, most are over 10 years old. We won't trade in a good, reliable piece of equipment.

I've lived here my whole life.

Shane VanderVeen

and fertilizers replaced the faith and hope that previously accompanied a relationship with the land? Does a theology and ethic undergird agribusiness and land use, or are these now "secular" activities?

I cannot begin to answer such questions, for the answers lie in the hearts of hundreds of individual farmers. But I do confess that I fret about it. I want to give testimony to a theology that unites faith and farming, the Creator of the universe with the Creator of science, the Lord of the Scriptures with land use in the 21st century.

Perhaps this can be best illustrated by the story behind the Whatcom Land Trust. Readers may be intrigued that this organization did not begin at Huxley College of Western Washington University, or as an offshoot of the Democratic Party, or the brainchild of an environmentalist from Fairhaven. Whatcom Land Trust was conceived in the basement of Dutch Mothers Restaurant in downtown Lynden.

In 1983, the Trust for Public Land contacted Concerned Christian Citizens, of which I was the director at the time. In cooperation with TPL, a forum was held that attracted approximately 50 people, including County Councilman Bob Muencher, Trillium Corp. founder David Syre, stewards like Hilda Bajema, attorneys like Rand Jack, farmers like Herman Miller. The chemistry of the group yielded commitments to continue the discussion; eventually Whatcom Land Trust was born. The ongoing success of the Land Trust has brought me considerable satisfaction during the past twenty years.

George Train, of Pleasant Valley Dairy on Kickerville Road, checks wheels of cheese as they cure. By increasing the value of their products, farmers and ranchers increase the likelihood that they will stay in business.
Photo: Manuel Rod del Pozo, courtesy of Farm Friends

A bounty of locally grown fruit and vegetables is available spring through fall in grocery stores, at produce stands, and at Bellingham Farmers Market. Some growers sell directly to consumers at their farms or through prepaid farm shares.
Photo: Steve Satushek

Every summer, the Northwest Washington Fair in Lynden offers
local youths a chance to showcase their farm animals and their
skills at husbandry.

Photo: Courtesy of The Bellingham Herald

These four photos show a portion of Johnson Creek on the Perry family farm southwest of Sumas that is being improved for salmon habitat through the Conservation Reserve Enhancement Program. The photo at far left shows the creek bed during the summer of 2000 followed by the same section that winter prior to replanting, then initial planting of native trees and shrubs in spring 2001 (left, page 85), followed by early growth of the plantings by summer 2001. Under the state-federal program, land owners stop farming and grazing along salmon waterways. In return, owners receive rental payments, and reimbursement for the creation and maintenance of buffers. As of May 2006, more than 1,500 acres in Whatcom County were involved, with 91 miles of buffer and nearly 750,000 seedlings planted.

Photos: Courtesy of Farm Friends

"Nature, to be commanded, must first be obeyed."

Sir Francis Bacon

But why would Lynden-based Concerned Christian Citizens be the origin of this movement? For that we need a quick lesson in history and theology. Though not founded by Dutch immigrants, Lynden was discovered by them around 1900. They brought with them a sturdy Calvinism that immediately gave birth to Reformed churches and, as early as 1910, Lynden Christian School. Their Calvinism emphasized the sovereignty of God over all of life, or as Dutch theologian and Prime Minister Abraham Kupyer once stated: "There is not one square inch of the entire creation about which Jesus Christ does not say 'This is mine! This belongs to me!'" Psalm 24 claims, "The earth is the Lord's, and the fullness thereof." The Creation was God's handiwork, and He placed Adam and Eve in the garden "to work it and take care of it" (Gen. 2:15). John Calvin, in a commentary on Genesis, taught: "Let him who possesses a field so partake of its yearly fruits, that he may not suffer the ground to be injured by his negligence, but let him

endeavor to hand it down to posterity as he received it, or even better cultivated…let everyone regard himself as a steward."

There you have it—a concept of stewardship. The Christian community rediscovered precisely that concept in the wake of the environmental crisis, and Christians of various stripes are seeking to live it out. A classic work, *Earthkeeping in the '90s: Stewardship of Creation*, was published in 1980, providing the theological and philosophical framework for applying Christian faith to ecological and environmental issues.

But has the "intellectual" framework for stewardship been brought down to the farm; has it infiltrated conversation in the coffee shops? Is it merely a worldview, and not yet a way of life? Has secularism won, so that we are practical atheists? What theology sits in today's tractor seat?

Oliver Wendall Holmes once spoke of a "simplicity on the other side of complexity." We started out with simplicity and moved toward the complexity of competing ideas, values and worldviews, the complexity of "progress." I wish for my community that we collectively find a second simplicity, a simplicity on the other side of complexity, a simplicity captured in another song (from that old songbook), and a prayer:

This is our Father's world: O let us not forget.
That though the wrong is great and strong, God is the ruler yet.
He trusts us with this his world, to keep it clean and fair—
All earth and trees, all skies and seas, all creatures everywhere.

Father, I pray for my community, all my friends and fellow citizens, that we will do justice to the land, to the creatures, to all. I pray for an ethic that will move us to be stewards of the earth. I pray for a grateful heart to appreciate this wonderful place in Creation called Whatcom County and the smaller part in it called Lynden.

Thank you for productive cattle and graceful horses that feed on and run through our pastures, and for all the lovely critters

Agriculture adds its own ordered beauty to Whatcom County.
Photo: Matt Brown

that make up the web of life. Thank you for corn chop-
pers and computer chips, these tools that you have given
to take away the drudgery of work. Thank you for the
geneticist, the chemist, the agronomist who uncover the
intricacies of Creation and use their knowledge to redeem
life and culture.

Father, if we have to build bigger barns, would it not be
for greed or ego! Would you prevent us from always bend-
ing our knee to the market, treating it like it is God. Would
you spare the family farm in this community.

Father, make us aware of any abuses we engage in,
polluting our water, spreading too much manure, using
too many chemicals. May we know when our profits are
enough, when we have worked enough, when we have
saved enough. Help us know if we have been negligent,
unobservant, disobedient.

Father, deliver us from any thought that we are on
our own, that you have deserted us, that we can do this
without you. We simply acknowledge you as the Creator
of "all things bright and beautiful, all creatures great and
small, all things wise and wonderful, Lord God, you made
them all." Amen.

At Pure Potato, in Lynden, varieties of seed
potatoes are developed for quality, nutrition, and
differing soil conditions.
Photo: Manuel Rod del Pozo, courtesy of Farm Friends

A worker plants seed potatoes near Lynden. Whatcom County is home to a
viable seed potato industry in which varieties of disease-free potatoes are
developed, grown, and then shipped to commercial potato growers.
Photo: Manuel Rod del Pozo, courtesy of Farm Friends

Photo: Manuel Rod del Pozo

"We need an environmental ethic that will tell us as much about using nature as about not using it… some kind of responsible use and non-use that might attain a balanced sustainable relationship."

William Cronon, *Uncommon Ground* (1996)

Green beans have been a staple crop for Whatcom County farmers for many decades. In recent years, organic green beans have taken hold, with about 900 acres of organic beans in production in 2006.

Photo: Manuel Rod del Pozo

Summer hay in the loft will feed Holstein cattle on this
Whatcom County dairy farm over the winter.

Photo: Jon Brunk

Hilda Bajema, activist
Photo: Ann Yow

The owl is a symbol of wisdom. This short-eared owl
(*Asio flammeus*), is the farmer's ally in helping to
control rodent populations.

Photo: Tim Fitzharris

*I've always looked to the outdoors for recreation with family
and friends all seasons of the year, but I've also used land for my
own purposes. I've raised vegetables and berries for family use,
and I became a farmer's wife.*

*Before marriage, I grew up in a small northern Maine town
surrounded by fields and forests. People earned a living by growing
potatoes, hay, and grain, operating dairy farms, logging,
and converting logs to firewood, lumber, and wooden dishes.
The land provided recreation for local people and tourists.*

*After moving to Whatcom County, my husband and I operated
a 60-acre dairy farm for 23 years. Upon retirement, we moved
to a three-quarter-acre property, where we had a small orchard
and a vegetable garden.*

*When I joined the League of Women Voters I studied land-use
planning and became involved for many years supporting legis-
lation to ensure sound land use at the local, state, and national
levels. Rand Jack and I served on the Whatcom County Land Use
Code Committee to develop a zoning ordinance for the county.*

*In 1983, when a group of citizens decided to protect valuable
farmland, I was appointed to a committee of six people to organize
what became the Whatcom Land Trust. I have served on the board
of directors since 1984, a very rewarding experience due to the
accomplishments and the people.*

Hilda Bajema

91

Urban paths like this one overlooking Bellingham Bay take on a
golden beauty each autumn.

Photo: Brett Baunton

An Urban Future

Aimee Frazier

Whatcom County's westernmost urban centers—Belling-ham, Ferndale, and Blaine—are bordered by an inland sea to the west and Interstate 5 on the east. These three burgeoning cities have the good fortune to also be surrounded by swaths of fertile farmland, the meandering ribbon of the Nooksack River, numerous lakes and streams, and, to the south, the Chuckanut Range, one of the few places on the planet where a sandstone mountain abuts the sea.

Geologic forces formed Bellingham and Birch Bays, built the Chuckanuts, and created a half dozen estuaries. Salmon spawned in now-urban streams for millennia; cougar, wolves, and bear roamed the valleys and lake shores; hundreds of species of birds, insects, plants, and trees lived among the hills. People from the Lummi, Samish, and Nooksack tribes fished, hunted, and resided near the water.

Change came after Henry Roeder arrived by Indian canoe and built a sawmill on Whatcom Creek in 1853. The settle-ment served as a stopover in the Fraser River gold rush, then slowly evolved into a frontier town. It seemed a most "forlorn and dilapidated" place in March 1870, when Phoebe Judson crossed a storm-swept Bellingham Bay in another Indian canoe, and journeyed up the Nooksack searching for her ideal

The old city hall, now the Whatcom Museum of History and Art, is a favorite landmark from land and water.
Photo: Manuel Rod del Pozo

Aimee Frazier lives on Pleasant Bay and is a full-time mother.

home. Fourteen years later, Whatcom County's venerable business, Morse Hardware, opened its doors.

In 1903, the two separate towns of New Whatcom and Fairhaven merged into one, named "Bellingham" (after Sir William Bellingham, who organized the provisions for English explorer Captain George Vancouver's 1792 voyage through the area). For the next century, hardy residents of this northwest corner would sustain themselves primarily through occupations dependent on land and sea: farming, fishing, and logging.

As Bellingham grew from a stopover town to a destination city, a burgeoning population imposed limits on land and resources, changing the way people lived and worked. In 1890, Bellingham's population was 8,135. By 1950 there were 34,112 residents, and 52,179 in 1990. In 2005, land that once supported the Lummi tribe was accommodating over 70,000 people. Bellingham's Planning Department forecasts nearly 113,000 will reside here by the year 2022. Blaine, Lynden and Ferndale are growing at an even faster rate, attracting many who seek a small-town atmosphere, beautiful views of farmland and mountains, and proximity to both Bellingham and Canada.

This steady influx of newcomers over the last century has brought inevitable growing pains. Resource extraction saw its limits as Whatcom County's waters were over fished and its forests cut. Jobs in heavy industry, higher education, health care, retail, and service jobs have supplanted resource industries as the current economic backbone of Whatcom County.

What draws newcomers to Bellingham, Ferndale, Lynden, Blaine? In the past 10 years, many national

The trail around Lake Padden is a popular route for walkers and joggers.
Photo: Jon Brunk

Located just east of Bellingham, Lake Whatcom provides drinking water, scenic beauty, and habitat for many animals, including deer.
Photo: Manuel Rod del Pozo

Lake Whatcom (foreground) and Bellingham Bay, two basins
gouged by ice-age glaciers, as seen from Stewart Mountain,
east of the city.

Photo: Grant Myers

Arroyo

When you stand near this creek alone,
listen to the faint lisp of currents
What will change by your presence,
What is concealed by your past,
Then imagine your own life over again,
those who have come and gone,
thoughts of what they wanted most
their pale fossilized glances
whirling by like juniper moths
spiraling toward some distant porch light—
this time of night it's okay to let go
this valley has waited long enough
for you to find trails to far off ridges;
you could spend a life here you know,
just standing in your own rim of thought
where nighthawks carve palisades
from a spray of evening hatches.

Matthew Campbell Roberts, Bellingham

The banana slug *(Aureolimax columbiansis)* is a familiar
northwest native.
Photo: Brett Baunton

The view of Chuckanut Creek in the densely forested Arroyo Park
provides refreshing respite for walkers of the Interurban Trail.
Photo: Gene Davis

magazines have cited Whatcom County as one of the most livable regions in the country. *National Geographic Adventure, Forbes, Money, AARP, Golf Digest, Sunset,* and other publications have praised Whatcom's air quality, its myriad outdoor recreation possibilities, its neighborhoods, schools, local flavor, bike-friendliness, and access to big-city arts and entertainment. In 2006 *Outside* magazine rated Bellingham as the nation's best paddling city. Whatcom County's celebrated reputation creates a number of conundrums: if many more are drawn to Bellingham, Ferndale, Lynden, and Blaine, will they retain their "livable-city" status? Will density destroy the very qualities those magazines highlight? How might overuse of the natural environment impact its biological integrity? These potential conflicts are addressed daily as local citizens anticipate and plan for the future.

To most residents, urban Whatcom County's quality of life depends on an abundance of green spaces and natural beauty. Bikers, walkers, and runners can travel miles through Bellingham on trails; snow enthusiasts, hikers, and technical mountaineers enjoy Mount Baker and the Cascades year-round; water lovers have access to numerous lakes and rivers, Bellingham Bay, and the San Juan Islands. In 1990, 1997, and again in 2006 Bellingham voters chose to tax themselves to establish and maintain the Greenways program. Revenue through the Greenways tax is used to purchase and maintain parks, trails, and recreation spaces throughout the city.

It is this love for Whatcom County's unique qualities that inspires city residents to preserve its local flavor and to protect the land. Many volunteer for organizations that work to protect local land and wildlife, such as

Bicyclists, runners, and walkers enjoy the Interurban Trail, a former rail line, which runs from south Bellingham to just south of Larrabee State Park on Chuckanut Drive.
Photo: Brett Baunton

Bellingham's Maritime Heritage Park brings spawning salmon up close to residents, including fishers.
Photo: Manuel Rod del Pozo

Whatcom Falls Park was created in 1908 when a private group, the Young Men's Commercial Club of Bellingham, raised money to buy 40 acres at a discount and then hold it until the land could be sold to the city. In time, the park grew to 214 acres. The stone bridge was built in 1939 using Chuckanut sandstone from a downtown building that was demolished after a fire.

Photo: Mark Turner

Jerry Eklund, retired refinery manager

Canadian Dogwood *(Cornus canadensis)* glistens after a rainfall.

Nowhere else in the world could be more enjoyable than what we have right here. Sometimes I had a hard time recruiting young engineers looking for bright lights and big city action, but proximity to Seattle and Vancouver enticed them, and once you got them here it was very difficult to get them to leave. It's the natural beauty, the diversity, a breathtaking landscape. In the flash of an eye you can go from water to skiing activities. People here are heavily in favor of outdoor activities, trails, and the environment. They proved that again by passage of the Greenways levy.

But keeping a balance with growth and development is a tough act. I have mixed emotions every day. Heavy industry, dirty industry, that's a conflict, and clearly not an easy one. Almost everybody acknowledges a need for more oil refining, but we don't want it here. Heavy industry also brings decent wages, but a new refinery would be virtually impossible with environmental restrictions what they are today, and rightly so.

What's most important to my wife and me in Whatcom County? There are so many pieces in my mind that I can't differentiate: it's the weather, it's the saltwater, the mountains and lakes, it's the environment, the greenery. All that stuff fits together, and I can't really put my finger on any single most important item. I believe all those things are important.

Jerry Eklund

Nooksack Salmon Enhancement Association, Northwest Wildlife Rehabilitation, Conservation Northwest, and RE Sources. Other locals lend time to nonprofits—such as Sustainable Connections and Whatcom Farm Friends—that support and encourage local businesses. Citizens work to provide affordable housing by volunteering with Kulshan Community Land Trust and address hunger issues through organizations like Small Potatoes Gleaning Project, Bellingham Community Meals, and the Bellingham Food Bank. Through volunteering for local nonprofits, many residents take to heart the words of Ivan Doig in this book's preface: "The ultimate experiencing of a sense of place comes from grounding our lives in such specific gifts of earth, and in having the sense to preserve them."

Whatcom, Chuckanut, Shuksan, Komo Kulshan, Nooksack, Samish—these native words tell of a time before "Bellingham" or "Baker." We newcomers can appreciate ancient life-ways on this western coast, yet we have different habits. Forests, mountains, rivers, and soil change decisively under our touch. Now is the time to ask: How much should we continue to radically alter this land, this beauty? What do we want our cities to look, sound, and feel like 10, 20, 50 years into the future?

Whatcom County's urban centers are at a crossroads, characterized by change and choices. Their desirability as places to live have brought numerous side effects: a dramatic increase in home prices, more traffic, crowded schools, and many dilemmas. How can we protect open space and farmland and also accommodate projected

Local farmers, bakers, flower growers, and crafts people are among those selling their wares at Depot Market Square, the new home for Bellingham Farmers Market, that opened in 2006.

Photo: Ginger Oppenheimer

Joe and Ann Bertero started Joe's Garden in south
Bellingham in the 1920s. Today, the operation remains a
viable business that's beautiful to behold.

Photo: Dick McNeely

Being a Stream

I will ask you to speak for me in your language, if only you sit quietly by my shores and listen. I will try to remember years I've endured; years are not in my language, but in yours. You see me only by daylight, the same light that has passed by for many lifetimes. Ask me if the earth might remember its creation. Ask me if the sun remembers its cold beginning of stellar dust and vapors. And will it know its cold death as it collapses inward generating more unknown space. Now ask me the way back to my beginning, the animals, and the peoples that have come and gone. There were days here before humans measured time. There was life before death in these waters of mine. I will tell you the stories of my life if you sit quietly by my shores in silence.

Matthew Campbell Roberts, Bellingham

Dozens of people gathered on a "Make a Difference Day" to uproot blackberries and plant trees along Whatcom Creek. Volunteers play an important role in restoring and maintaining the county's creeks, trails, and beaches.

Photo: Mark Turner

Elaine & Michael McRory, conservationists

Photo: Ann Yow

Cattails *(Typha latifolia)* conceal a nest of red-winged blackbird *(Agelaius phoeniceus)* eggs.

Photo: Steve Satushek

Elaine: Sometimes people live here their whole lives and never tune into what's being lost. That, in a nutshell, is why I became an "Enviro"—from observing gradual negative changes.

Mike: We used to fish 40 days of the year, trolling for salmon. As we had fewer and fewer fish, Elaine said, "Well, will we keep doing this until we catch the last fish?" We felt that if we're taking, we need to put something back. I got so excited by working on Connelly Creek, seeing fish in it, this tiny urbanized stream. And then I thought this might be done on a bigger scale, all over the county, bringing back wild salmon. So that was the beginning of NSEA.

We realized we could not do it alone. We don't blame anyone for the problem. All we want is to fix it and make things better. Now we have quite a volunteer force. Volunteers plant trees along a stream they didn't know existed. It suddenly has a name and they've seen fish in it. If they go back in 10 years, the tree is 30 feet tall and shading the creek. They see changes, which is encouraging and inspiring.

Elaine: At first some farmers really resisted. It was their land, a place for "raising crops, not fish." But they saw that a clean stream benefited them regardless of the fish, and now most farmers in the county are wonderful supporters.

Mike: Good water is vulnerable, but you can restore it if the damage hasn't gone too far. If people are committed, a degraded stream can be brought back to life.

Elaine: No one person has to do something really bad to cause a problem and the solutions are the same: no one has to go out and save the world. All they have to do is something. It's the cumulative effect that's important, both in destroying a resource and bringing it back.

Elaine & Michael McRory

population growth? Will communities choose to grow up via ever-taller buildings, or out, converting farmland and forests into urban areas? Can we utilize alternative means of transportation, alleviating congestion caused by cars? Will we support local businesses, or invite chain stores to occupy former farmland? How can we place limits on land surrounding our drinking water supply, while respecting the rights of private property owners? Differing answers to these questions have sometimes created divisiveness among residents who, being human, disagree on how to manage growth and its impacts. Continued dialogue, discussion, and collaborative compromise will be necessary as Whatcom County's urban centers surge into the future.

"Home, after all, is the place where finally we make our living. It is the place for which we take responsibility, the place we try to sustain so we can pass on what is best in it, and in ourselves, to our children."

William Cronon

Trails in Whatcom Falls Park provide a place to walk, run, bike, and to appreciate the beauty of nature.

Photo: Margaretha Maryk

Squalicum Lake, located a few miles east of Bellingham, drains
via a creek through dense residential, commercial, and industrial
areas into Bellingham Bay. Whatcom Land Trust places a high
priority on protecting urban open space and considers the
above scene a "highest and best use."

Photo: Manuel Rod del Pozo

Sunset casts a glow on Drayton Harbor at Blaine. Pollution and runoff have harmed oyster production in the harbor, but citizens and local governments have worked to restore the water quality and the once-bountiful shellfish.

Photo: Manuel Rod del Pozo

Jeralyn "Jeri" Smith, real estate agent

An icon of the Northwest, the great blue heron *(Ardea herodias)* thrives in lowlands where prime Whatcom County habitat supports the West Coast's largest breeding colonies.

I grew up at Birch Bay in a much simpler time. Peak population in winter was 300 people; summers would swell to several thousand. My mother ran a summer resort with 28 units. People didn't lock their doors; everyone knew you. You were raised by a village, really. We ran amok as kids through all the woods. Or fishing, we'd build rafts by the bay. Not until I went away as an adult did I pine for that beach. It's still my mental solace, to be on that beach. I have my early-morning coffee alone there.

I worry that this kind of specialness in Whatcom County will be erased and we will become just Anywhere-USA. Go to the East Coast on the freeway, pick any exit, and you find a place where people didn't care. And they lost it. Too often we don't pay attention to protecting our place until it's too late. We can lose the very qualities that attract people here in the first place.

When you see a threat to your home, you have to step up and speak out. You don't need to be obnoxious—obnoxious is totally counterproductive—but you need to be honest and truthful about what's right. And you can't wait. It won't do any good five years from now. Some of us are trying to preserve, protect, and enhance Birch Bay without paving it over and making it look like Miami Beach. We're really trying to avoid that.

Jeri Smith

Clark's Point, conserved by the family of Doug and Peggy Clark
in cooperation with Whatcom Land Trust, offers 71 acres of
beauty at the north end of Chuckanut Bay.

Photo: John Scurlock

The Land Ethic in Action: Voluntary Conservation

Dean Kahn

"This is a story about daring, where visionaries from a small land trust in Bellingham, Washington, formed critical partnerships and pulled out all the stops to preserve an ancient forest about to be sold for logging. When I visited… I was struck by how fully they embodied the qualities necessary to succeed against long odds: passion, vision, strategic thinking, tenacity, and just plain guts…"

from *Groundswell: Stories of Saving Places, Finding Community,* by Alix Hopkins, published by The Trust for Public Land (2005)

Private donors, local government, citizens and Whatcom Land Trust cooperated to create Canyon Lake Community Forest.
Photo: Roger Weiss

Whatcom County slumbered through the first half of the 20th century with a traditional blend of farming, logging, milling and fishing, plus its small state college high on a hill in Bellingham. That slumber stirred in the 1950s and awoke in the '60s with the arrival of oil refineries, an aluminum smelter, and baby boomer growth of the college. The same growth that brought new people who came to love the place also brought pressure on the region's remarkable beauty and fertile soil. By the early '80s, Concerned Christian Citizens, a local religious group based in Lynden, turned to focus on preserving farmland.

In the spring of 1983, the group convened a forum on the topic of land trusts. About 50 people gathered in the basement

"… to preserve and protect wildlife habitat, scenic, agricultural and open space land in Whatcom County for future generations by securing interests in land and promoting land stewardship."

Whatcom Land Trust Mission Statement

Dean Kahn is an editor and columnist with The Bellingham Herald.

The Miller farm is protected by a conservation easement.
Photo: Mark Turner

Easements and Conservation

Owning property brings a basket of rights accompanying the property—the right to build a house and rent it, to mine for gold, to plant or cut trees, to stop or permit access, to harvest crops, etc. Government can remove certain rights through zoning and regulations, and landowners can give away or sell their rights to others. Through a conservation easement, owners voluntarily transfer specific rights in order to conserve valuable features of their land. The easement is a private agreement in which a property owner gives a land trust carefully specified rights in order to protect open space, wildlife habitat, views, or fertile soil. The land trust then becomes the guardian of those rights, but by law cannot use them. An owner retains title to the land, which may be sold or left to heirs—but the restrictions remain "in perpetuity" regardless of ownership. For example, Herman and Diane Miller surrendered their right to subdivide their farm, add more houses, build a factory or parking lot, or create campgrounds. They preserved their right to live in their home, raise cattle, till the soil, sell milk and produce, and protect themselves from natural hazards.

of the popular Dutch Mothers restaurant. Among them were local business leaders, elected officials such as state Rep. Roger Van Dyken, an attorney named Rand Jack, and such farmers as Henry Polinder, Hilda Bajema, and Herman Miller.

Miller's Farm

It's a good thing Herman Miller wouldn't swallow the accepted legal wisdom about the future of his farm. A quiet, trusting man and a longtime farmer and horseman, Miller was born, raised, and happy on his 160-acre dairy farm east of Laurel. Yet he and his wife, Diane, watched nearby farms subdivide into small lots, and feared the same fate for their land. Miller talked with an attorney who told him that nothing could protect their acreage from sprouting houses. Learning about the idea of land trusts, the Millers attended the Dutch Mothers forum. They liked what they heard. A month later, when members of a fledgling committee met to pursue creation of a trust, Herman Miller was among them as a founder.

Whatcom Land Trust attained nonprofit status in 1984, but needed time to negotiate its first conservation easement with a property owner. On April 11, 1986, Herman and Diane Miller signed papers preserving their farmland forever. In more recent years, Whatcom County government has taken up the initiative to preserve farmland, to date spending $2.5 million to buy development rights on 325 acres of prime farmland. The Land Trust holds restrictive easements on the properties and monitors them to ensure compliance.

Such conservation can be seen as a tribute to Herman Miller's foresight. He died in December 2001. He and his wife were respected, solid citizens with deep roots in the community—a perfect couple to start a land trust on solid ground.

A Norwegian Homestead

Tom Nesset and his sister, Ingeborg, grew up east of Acme on a riverside farm that was settled by their Norwegian immigrant parents near the end of the 19th century. As a boy, Tom reacted with dismay when the hillside behind his home was stripped of large old-growth fir and cedar. He also watched Nooksack Indians catch and dry salmon on the nearby south fork of the river bearing their name, inspiring him and his brother George to place logs in Nesset Creek to improve spawning beds.

The late Herman Miller, one of the founders of Whatcom Land Trust.
Photo: Mark Turner

Tom Nesset (1898–1992), born in Norway, moved to his family's South Fork farm at age three and lived there for the rest of his life.
Photo: Rand Jack

Doug and Peggy Clark bought their stunning peninsula in 1958 and treated it with loving care.

Photo: Tore Ofteness

The Clark residence blends naturally into the landscape with a minimum of tree-cutting and is barely visible from the water or Chuckanut Drive.

Photo: Jonathan Duncan

Neither Tom nor Ingeborg had children, so there was no one to inherit their 106 acres. From time to time they discussed preserving the family land. A neighbor and distant cousin, Russ Pfeiffer-Hoyt, helped them tend the farm while endorsing their desire that it someday would become a park.

In 1989, shortly before Ingeborg died and three years before Tom's death, the two signed a conservation easement with Whatcom Land Trust that restricted logging on the hillside behind their house and provided for ultimate use of the land as a park.

Whatcom County bought the farm in 1998. Today, the future pioneer park still needs an access road and further restoration of its old buildings. The road will link Nesset farm with the Overby site purchased by the Trust, creating a park of nearly 600 acres and four miles of riverfront. It has the potential to be the finest county park in the state, perhaps the country. For that we can thank a Norwegian boy who, decades later, never forgot his dismay over the clear-cutting of a hillside.

Clark's Point

If the Miller farm put Whatcom Land Trust on the map and the Nesset farm extended its reach into the foothills, Clark's Point placed it firmly in the public eye. With conservation easements, as with home sales, location matters, and the location of Clark's Point near Chuckanut Drive has proven pivotal to the Land Trust's visibility.

Chuckanut Drive deserves its reputation as one of the most breathtaking stretches of road in the Northwest. The two-lane route lifts travelers north from the fertile flatlands of the Skagit delta and onto the shoulder of Blanchard and Chuckanut mountains before arriving in Bellingham. To the west lies Chuckanut Bay, dotted with islands, the flanks of Lummi Island and the San Juan Islands rising in the distance.

Near the northern opening of the bay, a small peninsula, forested and rocky, slopes to the south, its two fingers of land framing a narrow cove. Doug Clark, a former logger, a soldier at Normandy in 1944, and a pioneer Bellingham grocer, with his wife, Peggy, bought the peninsula plus 30 upland acres in

While many new homes have been built on Chuckanut Mountain, the number of houses allowed on Clark's Point is limited to only four, under a conservation agreement with Whatcom Land Trust.

Photo: Brett Baunton

1958. "It was rugged," he once recalled. "We just fell in love with it."

The Clarks built a modest home at the tip in 1961. As their son and two daughters reached adulthood, Doug and Peggy worried that someday their children would be pressured to sell the land for development. The parents wanted to preserve the peninsula for its beauty and its wildlife, but didn't want their children forced off the land by outside pressures.

In 1990, after many family sessions with Rand Jack, the Land Trust attorney and founding board member, the entire family endorsed a conservation easement for the 71 acres of Clark's Point. Fully developed, the point could accommodate at least 72 houses, perhaps more. The easement recognized four dwellings: one already built, two under construction at the time, and one later, with rules to limit their visual impact.

Peggy Clark, the driving force behind the agreement, died in 1998. Doug, who died seven years later, insisted that he and his wife "never regretted for a minute" protecting the forested treasure. That spirit was inherited: "I feel really honored to be a steward of the point," says Patrice Clark, one of their daughters. "I'm so proud of my parents' vision for this place."

A Jack of All Trades

In addition to conserving land through easements and outright purchase, Whatcom Land Trust also helps others reach conservation agreements. When that happens, you can be sure Rand Jack is involved.

In December 1987, Jack, who always volunteers his time, helped broker a complex deal to protect 112 steep,

Weathered sandstone offers fascinating shoreline patterns enjoyed by hikers and boaters with an eye for the art of nature.
Photo: Brett Baunton

Mike and Leslie Lebeau, newcomers

Photo: Ann Yow

Trumpeter swans *(Cygnus buccinator)* are stunning visitors to Whatcom County.

Photo: Fredrick Sears

Leslie: We're moving here because Whatcom County is beautiful and she still has her own ecological character and natural graces.

Living here will enable us to spend time in nature. There is a felt sense of sacred place here. Nature is very much my church. I love to walk into the woods or along the shore, to kayak and see wildlife. To me, it's the presence of God. I couldn't survive, spiritually, without it.

Mike: The Bellingham area still has large and vibrant natural areas, places able to speak to people, to inspire a response from our souls and spirits. It certainly does that for us.

Leslie: I grew up in the Santa Clara Valley when it was an enormously wild and agricultural place. I walked to school through orchards and meadows and across a creek. I cut and picked fruit in the orchards near my home for summer money. Then every acre was bulldozed and developed. In Whatcom County, every piece of land, every tree, isn't just about economics.

Mike: Conservation is heartfelt, and must be an exercise in community-building to be successful in the long run. As a community we receive the benefits.

Leslie: Yes, we bought land here limited by a conservation easement. The easement provides a buffer, a walking area, a sanctuary for wildlife. Participating in stewardship of something so precious is meaningful to us. It's amazing that places such as Clark's Point exist, and we appreciate the generosity of the Clark family and the sacrifice they made to protect it.

Mike and Leslie Lebeau

Voluntary Conservation

Conservation Futures levy money from Whatcom County and
a large private donation through Whatcom Land Trust enabled
the county to acquire Squires Lake Park. A conservation
easement ensures a light touch by humans.

Photo: Mark Turner

forested acres on Lummi Island that provided roost for endangered peregrine falcons. A Texas businessman who owned the site planned to develop it. With Jack's help, seven different parties agreed to a $478,000 sale that resulted in the state Department of Fish and Wildlife protecting the falcons. Funding came from the state and a private donor.

In 1993, Jack changed the western profile of Whatcom County by negotiating a mammoth land exchange involving two state agencies, Whatcom County, Bellingham, and the Trillium Corp., owned by Whatcom County native David Syre. In the end, Trillium and the state swapped nearly 33 square miles of forest land, with the state Department of Natural Resources acquiring nearly 11 square miles in Lake Whatcom watershed, the source of drinking water for more than 86,000 residents.

Larrabee State Park added 800 acres on Chuckanut Mountain, while county parks eventually received the 260-acre Syre homestead along the south fork of the Nooksack River. In a related deal, the public gained 400 acres along the crest of the Chuckanuts, perhaps the most spectacular lowland view site in Northwest Washington.

Over that ridge, east of Interstate 5, Jack persuaded local families, two county governments, an anonymous donor and a half-dozen business firms to create Squires Lake Park. After conferring with Jack and a real estate agent, the owner of the property agreed to sell it for half the asking price. A jack-of-all-trades—and sales.

The trail around Squires Lake provides close views of freshwater plants.

Photo: Mark Turner

A gentle trail through Canyon Lake Community Forest lets hikers appreciate one of the oldest stands in the Pacific Northwest, with some trees over 800 years old.

Photo: Chris Moench

After Canyon Lake Community Forest was created, the original property owner, Crown Pacific Timber Co., graciously returned a 50-million-year-old fossil palm frond for display at the main trailhead.

Photo: Helen Scholtz

Canyon Lake Community Forest

As part of the 1993 land exchange, Trillium Corp. agreed to consider preservation of 350 acres of old-growth forest above Canyon Lake in the foothills east of Deming. David Syre granted a purchase option to the national Trust for Public Land, an option that carried over in 1997 when Trillium sold the property to Crown Pacific Timber Co. of Portland, Oregon.

A University of Washington forestry scientist hired to assess the stand of trees discovered to his astonishment that some yellow cedars had reached 800 years, making the creek basin one of the most ancient standing forests in the Pacific Northwest. Cloud cover and moisture had buffered the cedars, mountain hemlocks and silver firs from forest fires, while steep slopes had deterred loggers.

Learning this, Crown Pacific increased the sale option to 750 acres in the upper basin. The Trust next brought in Bill Pope, representing Paul Allen's forest protection foundation. Hiking old logging roads, he gazed over the 45-acre lake and the ancient forest, then encountered stunning views of Mount Baker and the Twin Sisters from a high ridge. Smitten, Pope challenged his hosts: "You guys are thinking too small. You should buy this entire basin, all 2,300 acres of it." Allen's foundation did its part with a $1.8 million grant, while two private donors combined for another $1.3 million. That left the Trust $700,000 short as the November 1993 option deadline drew near.

After a front page article in *The Seattle Times*, editorial support from *The Bellingham Herald*, endorsements

A natural slide created Canyon Lake, visible from the trail to a ridge that
offers spectacular views of Mount Baker and the Twin Sisters.
The area's beauty inspired major private donations that made
acquisition and preservation of the basin possible.

Photo: Mark Turner

from local businesses and loggers, and some astute lobbying by Rand Jack, the County Council agreed to fund the balance. Today, Whatcom County is part owner of Canyon Lake Community Forest. Western Washington University shares ownership of the land, used as a site for scientific research. Whatcom Land Trust holds a conservation easement on the property.

After sealing the deal, Crown Pacific donated the conversion of a logging road into a trail. The company also returned a fossil palm frond removed years earlier. Standing six feet high, five feet across, and weighing six tons, the 50-million-year-old stone today greets hikers ascending the forest trail above the lake.

Salmon, Eagles, and Herons

Protecting land generally protects wildlife as well, but some transactions have specific creatures in mind. Example: the 300 pairs of birds that make Birch Bay Great Blue Heron Colony one of the largest on the West Coast. In 1996, ARCO Products Co. at Cherry Point signed a conservation easement on 77 acres to protect the colony. Three years later, the ARCO refinery donated another easement on 103 adjacent acres. Then in 2005, the county, state and BP (the site's new owner) agreed to buy 15 platted acres to further buffer the herons.

In 2002, eagles and eagle-watchers were winners when Whatcom Land Trust received 33 acres of popular eagle territory for a new county park. Hank and Lorrell Rensink donated their family land near the three branches of the Nooksack River. It was a fitting gift. Hank wears eagle hats and T-shirts, and his home is filled with pictures of eagles. For Hank's 50th birthday, his son baked him a cake decorated with a frosting-eagle.

Bald eagles *(Haliaeetus leucocephalus)* frequent the Nooksack River as a place to feed and nest. Eagle-watching is a popular activity for visitors as well as local residents.

Photo: Marcy Bloomenthal

Eagles love salmon, and salmon need protection, too—especially spring chinook, an endangered species of the Nooksack. In one of his many efforts to assist salmon, Land Trust conservation director Gordon Scott acquired a state grant to buy 443 acres along the river's north fork. That protected 2.7 miles of prime spawning habitat, the largest salmon conservation project in Whatcom County history. Local Indian tribes and the Nooksack Salmon Enhancement Association, founded by Michael and Elaine McRory, helped restore the habitat.

In an innovative maneuver, the state Department of Transportation donated to the Land Trust 68 acres where Maple Creek enters the north fork of the Nooksack as compensation for damage to salmon habitat during emergency road repairs on Mount Baker Highway. In that deal, as in many salmon projects, "persistence" became Gordon Scott's middle name.

A Forest in a City

Concern about the purity of Lake Whatcom water has increased as more homes rise in the watershed. In one response, the city of Bellingham now buys undeveloped parcels to prevent future runoff. But private individuals have taken action, too.

In 2000, the seven children of physician Edward K. Stimpson and his wife, Catharine C. "Kitty" Stimpson, donated 116 acres to Whatcom Land Trust. That became the core of the Stimpson Family Nature Reserve. A family grandfather, Arthur Watts, had bought the logging camp property in the early 1900s. No houses or other structures existed on it, just trees, trails, creeks, and a beaver pond to serve as a rustic outdoor area for the

Some of Whatcom Land Trust's protected lands provide elk habitat. Local tribes and the State are working to restore the herds in the county.
Photo: Fredrick Sears

A three-mile trail at Stimpson Family Nature Reserve offers calming enjoyment of the forested site above Lake Whatcom.
Photo: Bob Butterfield

These intertwining trees can be seen from the trail at Stimpson Family Nature Reserve.

Photo: Mark Turner

Stimpson family. After Edward and Kitty Stimpson died, the seven siblings discussed how to best use the land. The idea of development intrigued some, but all eventually agreed that an urban forest was not theirs to alter. "Mom just wanted to keep the place the way it was," recalls Susan Trimingham, one of the daughters. "We had a desire to give it to the community."

The family's donation triggered other transactions that multiplied the public benefit. Whatcom County paid the Land Trust $500,000 for the Stimpson conservation and recreation easements, on condition the Land Trust use the money to acquire adjacent acreage and establish an endowment to build and maintain three miles of trail. Western Washington University donated two small parcels nearby, and the state Department of Natural Resources designated a 138-acre conservation site as part of the Stimpson reserve, which now covers 350 acres, a genuine forest only a few minutes' drive from the center of Bellingham. "It was a great example of private and public and educational institutions all coming together," says Trimingham. "We're glad our donation could start that process."

Small Properties, Big Benefits

In most cases, property owners approach Whatcom Land Trust about the idea of protecting their land for future generations. And in most cases, the land involved is small, from a fraction of an acre to fewer than 50 acres, far smaller than the headline-grabbing transactions involving hundreds, even thousands, of acres.

An example: Western Washington University art professor Ruth Kelsey designed her own home in

Bellingham, but bought 20 acres near Lake Terrell Wildlife Refuge west of Ferndale, thinking that she might want to live in the countryside. She changed her mind, but often walked on and picnicked at the property, and sometimes rented the fields to cattle grazers. In 1992, her health failing, she donated the 20 acres to the Land Trust. The state now manages the property along with the wildlife refuge. Kelsey died eight years after she donated the land. Her legacy lives on in her art, her land, and in several college scholarships she started.

Another example: in 2006, California real estate developer Mike McCormack donated to the Land Trust a two-acre rocky headland and saltwater lagoon below the Madrona Pointe subdivision he developed in south Bellingham. The land, with 1,200 feet of shoreline cliff and a five-acre lagoon, is one of the few stretches of Bellingham Bay untouched by industrial or residential development.

A few months later Nate and Phyllis Kronenberg donated an easement on their 30-acre forest south of Everson. "We've sort of become part of the land," Nate reflected, "We've become one with all the big trees."

That same spring in 2006, Don and Judith Jensen worked with the Land Trust to establish a 23-acre forest park on their 270-acre diary farm near the Birch Bay-Lynden Road. During the Depression of the 1930s, Don had protected young firs from Christmas tree hunters. He explained why in a few words: "I just liked trees." The Jensen forest with its centuries-old Douglas-firs became another park created through cooperation between Whatcom County and the Land Trust.

A gift of property to Whatcom Land Trust protects the rugged coastline and forested uplands at Pigeon Point. Taylor Shellfish Company owns and farms the tidelands.

Photo: Eric Carabba

Lush growth abounds on the 17-acre Zweegman property on Birch Point, where a conservation easement preserves habitat for nesting bald eagles.

Photo: Eric Carabba

Spring Fogelsong, nine years old

Photo: Manuel Rod del Pozo

I like being outside because I feel more free. Plus, you can do more running. And I like being wild, that's for sure. I wish I could live with more trees and woods and forests. More wild. That's what I like.

I'd like to see more parks where people can come and see wild animals living their life. I like bears and sea animals. I like insects, crickets that play music. That's nice. Animals are just like people, living things that we need to consider and take care of. If one species of animal goes out, you break a big web of life and it's really hard on the other life. And then everything might die. That won't work. Even in the water—if things in the water die, then things on the land will die. That's the problem. And even trees might die.

Another reason I like animals is because they're really beautiful. They all have good ways of protecting themselves, getting what they need to live. I think that's one of the most amazing things about animals.

Spring Fogelsong

The elusive black bear *(Ursus americanus)* once ranged from lowlands to mountains, but now is rarely seen away from highlands. Bears symbolize wilderness and play a key role in the ecosystem of the Cascade Mountains.

Photo: Jon Timmer

In 1998, Evelyn Nieuwendorp agreed to a conservation easement with
Whatcom Land Trust for 8.7 acres of fields and wetlands next to Lynden
on the north side of the Nooksack River. The easement protects habitat
and provides a buffer by the river against development.

Photo: Mark Turner

For Future Generations

Through mid-2006, Whatcom Land Trust in 20 years had initiated 10 new county parks. The Trust owned 52 properties totaling over 2,000 acres, and held conservation easements on another 41 parcels covering more than 4,700 acres. Together, that's more than 10 square miles of special lands preserved forever—10 square miles for which the future can say "thank you" to families like the Millers, Nessets, Clarks, Rensinks, and Stimpsons, to businesses such as BP, ARCO, and Trillium, to our city and county governments, and to the many individuals such as Rand Jack who volunteer hours of their time to conserve the beauty of Whatcom County.

With rapid development and population growth now occurring in the county, the 800 members of the Land Trust, its dedicated staff, and their network of supporters will continue to play a vital role protecting important scenic, wild, and agricultural places. One can confidently predict more instances of what Maine author Alix Hopkins encountered when she interviewed Land Trust members who created Canyon Lake Community Forest: "You sense the passion, daring, and tenacity of a group of people with diverse but ultimately common interests, who came together to ensure [this forest's] preservation for everyone, forever."

"People's lives are immediately diminished whenever their connections with an elemental environment are blurred or broken."

Benton McKay, *The New Exploration* (1920)

Land restoration work, such as tree planting, requires the effort of dedicated volunteers.
Photo: Gordon Scott

An old stump provides support and nutrients for another tree, one forest example of the circle of life.
Photo: Eric Carabba

Whatcom Land Trust property off the Rutsatz Road contains
prime salmon and elk habitat. The river frontage was restored
in cooperation with the Lummi and Nooksack tribes.

Photo: Gordon Scott

Whatcom Place Names

Robert Keller

"How a particular culture or subculture divides and names the features of its homescape…is in the end peculiar to that culture. Thus, it's hard to be certain about what someone else's word for something might be. Or even what that word might mean.

We [name land] intentionally, to make what is separate from us part of where we are. We put a geometry to the land…and pick out patterns in it… It is a language that keeps us from slipping off into abstract space."

Barry Lopez, speaking at Village Books, October 4, 2006

Names help define the meaning of products, people and places. If we call a peninsula "Governors Point" instead of "Rugged Point," we not only think about it differently, but we see it differently. Not surprisingly, names also change over time as the residents and their cultures change: Northwest natives would never have used the words "disappointment," "discovery," or "flattery" for capes along the Washington coast. In Whatcom County, such names as "Cordata" and "Fairhaven Parkway" are of recent origin.

The following names are only a few dozen of hundreds that define place in our county. Most of these sites, and many more, once had Samish, Skagit, Nooksack or Lummi names with vastly different meanings—a fascinating study for the future. Origin and definition, whether for native languages or in English, often remain unclear or controversial.

Names change.

"Until I was thirty, I wanted to save the world. Between the ages of thirty and sixty, I wanted to save the country. But since I was sixty, I've wanted to save the Indiana Dunes."

U.S. Senator Paul Douglas

In the Northwest, our "dunes" are natural treasures like Chuckanut Bay.

Photo: Jon Brunk

Acme: *From the Greek word for "top," here it derives from a hymnal once used in the village.*

Bellingham: *Admiral Peter Rainier never saw the mountain and Sir William Bellingham never saw the bay that British explorer George Vancouver in 1792 would name.*

Birch Bay: *Vancouver, anchoring here, observed black birch trees along the shore.*

Blaine: *James G. Blaine was James Garfield's secretary of state and ran for president in 1884.*

Bloedel-Donovan Park: *Julius Bloedel logged and mined in the Lake Whatcom watershed; J. J. Donovan, an engineer, arrived in Bellingham during the late 1880s to work on rail construction and the Nooksack Falls powerhouse.*

Blue Canyon: *While hiking near Lake Whatcom, early business tycoon James F. Wardner, reportedly sober, noticed a blue tinge at a potential lode of coal.*

Berthusen Park: *In 1889, Norwegian immigrant Hans Berthusen married Lida Hawley of Lynden. After he died in 1944, their estate left this stand of ancient trees to the city.*

Carter Point: *Petty Officer William Carter served with Charles Wilkes U.S. Exploring Expedition, 1838–1842.*

Cascade Range: *Explorer Manuel Quimper called it* Sierra Nevada de San Antonio. *Vancouver referred to the mountains as snowy, while Lewis and Clark spoke of western mountains. The origin of "Cascade" remains unclear.*

Chilliwack: *The native word translates as "to go up river as far as possible in a canoe."*

Chuckanut: *A "bay with forest fire or burn" refers to the frequently burned western side of the range.*

Clark's Point: *The forested peninsula was purchased by Doug and Peggy Clark in 1958 (See pages 108, 112–114).*

Over a century ago such leaders as Grover Cleveland and Theodore Roosevelt created our national forest legacy.

Photo: Steve Satushek

In 2000 a Bellingham family donated private land to begin an
urban forest legacy inside the city.

Photo: Bob Butterfield

Before Sunrise

Saturday
before sunrise
walking over leaf layered ground
through woods
saturated with silence
the familiar a bit sinister
in this crepuscular light.

Ferns, foliage
fir trees and cedars
creatures of a dark dreamscape.
Fog floats, glides
weaves around trees
shape shifters, spirits
a liminal world.

I walked entranced
inhabited
my belly big with stillness
my breath a silver ghost.

Lillian Palermo, Lummi Island

Snow geese (*Chen hyperborea*) fill the sky.
Photo: Steve Satushek

Clipper: The name survives from the Clipper Shingle Co.

Custer: Albert Custer, postmaster and storekeeper, lived here in the 1880s.

Deming: George Deming served as the town's first postmaster.

Diablo: Originally, it referred to a turbulent, unnavigable canyon on the upper Skagit River, then this Spanish word for "devil" was applied to a Seattle City Light dam construction site.

Drayton Harbor: Joseph Drayton, an artist, served on the Wilkes U.S. Exploring Expedition.

Eliza Island: Spanish explorer Francisco Elisa, later misspelled as Eliza, sailed past the island in 1791.

Everson: The first white settler in the area was Ever Everson, a Norwegian.

Ferndale: Alice Eldridge selected the name in 1876. She was the first teacher at a one-room log schoolhouse by a fern patch.

Grant Peak: The summit of Mount Baker was named in 1869 for Ulysses S. Grant, victorious Union general and newly elected U.S. president. Grant's wartime colleague Gen. William Tecumseh Sherman is recognized nearby at **Sherman Peak** and **Sherman Crater**.

Hale Passage: Horatio Hale sailed with the world-circumnavigating Wilkes Expedition.

Hannegan Pass: Thomas Hannegan, director of the Washington State Road Commission, inspected the pass for an east/west route in 1893.

Hinote's Corner: Ben and Myrtle Hinote owned the store at the Hannegan/Pole Road intersection, 1925–1966.

Hovander Park: Hokan and Leontine Hovander consolidated old land claims to create a farm.

Kendall: Carthage Kendall from Virginia settled here in 1884.

King Tut Road: Constructing the road coincided with the discovery of a famous mummy in Egypt.

Kulshan: The word means "shooting place," or a steep hunting area. The Nooksack name for Mount Baker is Komo Kulshan.

Great blue heron (*Ardea Herodias*).
Photo: Patrick Reeves

"We need another and a wiser and perhaps a more mystical concept of animals. Remote from universal nature, and living by complicated artifice, man in civilization surveys the creature through the glass of his knowledge and sees thereby a feather magnified and the whole image in distortion. We patronize them for their incompleteness, for their tragic fate of having taken form so far below ourselves. And therein we err, and greatly err. For the animal shall not be measured by man. In a world older and more complete than ours they move finished and complete, gifted with extensions of the senses we have lost or never attained, living by voices we shall never hear. They are not brethren, they are not underlings; they are other nations, caught with ourselves in the net of life and time, fellow prisoners of the splendour and travail of the earth."

From *The Outermost House* by Henry Beston (1928)

A waterfall at Squires Lake Park, a quiet sanctuary above I-5. Whatcom Land Trust acquired the lake in 1995.

Photo: Brett Baunton

Kwina: *Teenager Henry Kwina attended the 1855 treaty council at Mukilteo.*

Lake Terrell: *N. G. Terrell surveyed the area in the late 1850s.*

Larrabee: *Charles Larrabee bought large tracts of land in Fairhaven during the late 1880s. After his death in 1915, family heirs created Washington's first state park in his memory.*

Lummi: *Native tradition tells of families with this name moving from Lopez Island to Gooseberry Point. They dominated the islands as well as nearby shorelines in the late 1700s and early 1800s.*

Lynden: *Phoebe Judson drew upon a poem,* Hohenlinden, *to name the town in 1870.*

Mount Baker: *Vancouver named it after Lt. Joseph Baker, who, in 1792, sighted the peak. Spanish explorer Manuel Quimper (1790) had called it* La Gran Montaña del Carmelo.

Newhalem: *Newhalem Creek joined the Skagit at a village site. The Indian word may mean "goat snare."*

Nooksack: *"Always bracken fern roots" is a traditional translation.*

Nugent's Corner: *1880s homesteader Peter Nugent operated a river ferry near the present bridge crossing. Others say the name came from Henry Nugent, an early 20th century grocer in the area.*

Padden: *Coal miner Michael Padden settled at the confluence of Padden and Connelly creeks.*

Point Migley: *William Migley was a gunner with Wilkes in 1841.*

Point Roberts: *Henry Roberts had earlier commanded Vancouver's ship* Discovery.

Point Whitehorn: *Daniel Whitehorn was another gunner on the Wilkes Expedition.*

Roeder: *Many street names come from the Roeder family:* Elizabeth, Victor, Henry *and* Lottie. *Henry Roeder arrived to speculate in land three years before the 1855 treaty.*

Ross Lake/Ross Dam: *The dam, once known as Ruby Dam, was re-named in 1939 for Seattle City Light Superintendent James D. Ross, who is further memorialized by a rock crypt at Newhalem, the long reservoir and a mountain.*

Ruth Mountain: *President Grover Cleveland, who in 1897 initiated the future Mount Baker National Forest, had a daughter, Ruth.*

Samish: *The name is associated with native people who lived in what is now Skagit and Whatcom Counties.*

Saxon: *Elizabeth Saxon, a passionate crusader against liquor, purchased dry South Fork land in 1888.*

Sefrit: *Frank I. Sefrit, a mountain climber, published* The Bellingham Herald, *1911–1950.*

Sehome: *1855 treaty signer Sehome was related to Clallam, Samish and Lummi tribes through descent and marriages.*

Semiahmoo: *The name is associated with native people who lived in the area.*

Shuksan: *The original meaning remains unclear; it's possibly derived from "high up" and "foot."*

Skagit: *Named after the Skagit people, the river flows south from British Columbia through eastern Whatcom County.*

Sumas: *The Cowichan word describes a "big level opening."*

Tennant Lake: *John Tennant settled here in 1858.*

Van Zandt: *Dutch newcomer J. M. Van Zandt filed a land claim in 1883.*

Welcome : *John Welcome Riddle became postmaster in the late 1880s.*

Whatcom: *In 1852, the first town on Bellingham Bay was named after "loud or roiling water."*

Wickersham: *In 1885, Noah and William Wickersham reached the south end of Lake Whatcom, then traveled overland to the Nooksack River and staked out property.*

Wiser Lake: *In the 1870s, Jacob Wiser filed a cash claim at a pond once known as Goose Lake.*

The classic study of American geographic language is George R. Stewart's *Names on the Land* (Houghton Mifflin Co., 1945). Coverage of our state is in James W. Phillips, *Washington State Place Names* (University of Washington Press, 1976). For the story of many modern names given during exploration, see Edmond S. Meany, *Vancouver's Discovery of Puget Sound* (Binfords & Mort, 1957) and Nathaniel Philbrick, *Sea of Glory* (Viking, 2003). For topographic names beyond place, see Barry Lopez, *Home Ground: Language for an American Landscape* (Trinity University Press, 2006). We thank Tim Wahl of the Bellingham Parks & Recreation Department for advice on many of these entries.

Skunk cabbage and beaver flourish along Innis Creek, a tributary of the Samish River. Whatcom Land Trust purchased the 50 acres in 2004 with state salmon recovery funds.

Photo: Eric Carabba

WHATCOM LAND TRUST
Preserving the *Nature* of Whatcom County

98 Central Ave., Bellingham, WA   98225
Phone: **360-650-9470**
Fax: **360-650-0495**
E-mail:
info@whatcomlandtrust.org
website:
www.whatcomlandtrust.org

Production Notes

Design: **Roderick C. Burton–Art & Design**

Body text and headlines are set in Minion, captions and credits are Syntax, supplementary type is Ellington.

Scanning/Image optimization: **Artscan**

Scanning done using a Scanview Drum scanner and Nikon Film scanner

Printing: **Lithtex NW**

Printed with vegetable-based inks on Knightkote Matte 100# text with matching cover. Recycled content: 50% (30% post-consumer waste)

Delicate maidenhair fern *(Adiantum pedatum)* flourishes in the rich, moist soil of Whatcom County.

Photo: Gloria Ruyle

Back Flap: An annual festival celebrates the uses and fragrant beauty of lavender grown on Lummi Island.

Photo: Margaretha Maryk

Inside Back Cover: Whatcom County showing protected lands.

Map: Chris Behee

This Douglas-fir *(pseudotsuga menziesii)* graces the Stimpson Family Nature Reserve. The family's donation of 116 forested acres above Lake Whatcom triggered other donations, purchases and agreements that resulted in a 350-acre preserve.

Photo: Brett Baunton